Praise for *InstaGrateful*

"No other motivational book explores the profound effects of social media on our self-image and self-worth. With *InstaGrateful*, Sheri Fink delivers powerful strategies and tools for taking control of our dreams and destiny, and living more authentic and fulfilling lives, both online and offline."

   -Eve Torres Gracie, co-creator of the Women Empowered self-defense program

"As a parent of a 10-year-old girl navigating the waters of social media for good, best-selling author Sheri Fink's latest book *InstaGrateful* is not only an empowering resource for women and young girls on how to live authentically and safely share their light in the online world, but an inspiring guide for the next generation of ladies longing to be role models as well."

   -Brooke Josephson, singer-songwriter, wife, and mom

"Every once in a while, you read a book that transforms the way you think about your life, igniting within you the motivation to create the reality that you most deeply desire. This is that book."

   -Kate Linder, *The Young and the Restless*

"With *InstaGrateful,* Sheri Fink has created a heartfelt, dynamic, and practical rendering of how to live a fulfilled, meaningful, and intentional life. She shares her experiences and wisdom in a spirit of service and thus provides a true navigation towards excellence and inner peace."

   -Ranj Bawa, life coach and speaker

"A wonderfully written book by Sheri Fink! Her passion for helping others on this path of life shines through. Sheri takes you by the hand and leads you through valuable lessons for life. Sharing her own stories of success and failure means you connect with the lesson and can translate the meaning easily into your own world. Imagine a big sister sharing her wisdom when you need it most."

   -Amanda Brown, speaker, coach, and author of *The LIPSTICK Principles:*
       Let go of worry and fear, live in the moment, love life

"Sheri Fink is a true role model. There's nothing more powerful than honing your voice and story to create positive change. Packed with inspirational takeaways from her personal experiences, *InstaGrateful* will take you on a journey towards connecting with the authentic you in our social-media-driven world."
-Suhani Parikh, author and founder of Modern Marigold Books

"Sheri inspires you to take an 'Insta-inside' look of who you truly are and turn it into an 'Insta-outside' picture of your authentic self to present to the world."
-Renée Lawless, *Wicked* on Broadway and Tyler Perry's *The Haves and the Have Nots*

"*InstaGrateful* is part personal change manifesto, part memoir, and all heart. Sheri Fink has a fresh and unique voice in the motivational community, one that's full of uplifting humor, pure joy, and powerful insights for our modern times. There's wisdom and inspiration on every page of this soon-to-be motivational classic."
-Cheryl Bonini Ellis, author, speaker, and high-performance leadership coach

"Through *InstaGrateful,* Sheri Fink empowers all of us to blossom into our most passionate, peaceful, powerful, prosperous, and panache-filled selves. This is a must read!"
-Amy Leigh Mercree, international speaker and best-selling author of *Joyful Living, The Mood Book,* and *100 Days to Calm*

"Sheri Fink's *InstaGrateful* leaves you with a smile while you read it. Sheri gives us a fresh and unique voice in the inspirational community, one that's full of uplifting humor, authenticity, and genuine heart. Her strategies aren't just informative— they're effective and empowering. If you're committed to creating the life of your dreams, Sheri's voice will support you to be fearless for what you want."
-Jill Douka, MBA, MCC, life coach, award-winning business mentor, and best-selling author of *Create Love*

"Sheri has done it again! *InstaGrateful* is a powerfully positive book featuring transformational strategies that will up-level countless women's lives."
-Lanette Pottle, life and business strategist, and founder of Positivity Lady Enterprises

"Empowering. Inspiring. Evolutionary. *InstaGrateful* is an essential read for women who are seeking bliss and meaning in our social media world. Chapter after chapter of uplifting stories and gentle nudging for us to embrace joy and purpose. A definite must read."
-Cheryl Liew, author of *The 24-Hour Woman: How High Achieving, Stressed Women Manage It All and Still Find Happiness,* proud mom of three boys, and CEO of LifeWorkz

"*InstaGrateful* contains powerful, inspiring, and authentic real-life strategies that up-level women's lives."
-Lakshmi Kumar, beacon of light and love, wife, and mother

"For years, Sheri Fink has been inspiring children to dream big and live authentically. Now, the adults who have enjoyed planting Sheri's seeds of wisdom and kindness in their children's hearts and minds through her amazing children's books have more powerful inspiration of their own—*InstaGrateful* is a must-read for any woman who yearns to find solace in their perfectly imperfect world despite the perfectly painted pictures of life across social media platforms. An in-depth look at how Sheri found courage to truly shine her inner light—and how you can shine unwaveringly, too."
-Danielle Soucy Mills, award-winning author, gymnastics coach, and mom

"Sheri Fink shares her own personal and inspirational story to teach the five Ps that every woman should live by in today's busy world."
-Kathryn Starke, founder of Creative Minds Publications

"*InstaGrateful* contains priceless jewels of insight and sound strategies to make your dreams come true. Sheri's *InstaGrateful* will give you an essential roadmap for developing internal strength and balance in order to live the life of your dreams in this social media world."
-Juliet "Jhet" van Ruyven, mentor, inspirational speaker, and best-selling author

"Sheri Fink is an extraordinary woman accomplishing extraordinary feats. I'm blown away by her clarity in thought and ability to break down complex ideas into simple, yet powerful metaphors. *InstaGrateful* is a catalyst for changing the way we view ourselves and living a bold, balanced, and blissful life."

-Puja Gupta, life coach and author

"InstaGrateful is transformational! The powerful strategies are infused with self-care, self-love, and a never-give-up attitude sure to accelerate women's success."

-Deborah Lucero, best-selling author and founder of Live Your Full Life

To Becky -
A beautiful
lotus!

InstaGrateful

FINDING YOUR BLISS IN A
SOCIAL MEDIA WORLD

SHERI FINK

Inspirational Speaker and #1 International
Best-selling Author of *The Little Rose*

INSTAGRATEFUL: FINDING YOUR BLISS IN A SOCIAL MEDIA WORLD By Sheri Fink

Library of Congress Control Number: 2020908872
ISBN: 978-1-949213-15-7

Printed in China

FIRST EDITION

For my fellow Lotus Flowers: It's your time to bloom.

"Like a lotus flower, we too have the ability to rise from the mud, bloom out of the darkness, and radiate into the world." ~ *Unknown*

Books by Sheri Fink:

The Little Rose
The Little Gnome
The Little Firefly
Exploring the Garden with the Little Rose
The Little Seahorse
Counting Sea Life with the Little Seahorse
The Little Unicorn
World of Whimsy with the Little Unicorn
The Little Dragon
Cake in Bed
*My Bliss Book: An Inspirational Journal for Daily Dream Building and
Extraordinary Living*
InstaGrateful: Finding Your Bliss in a Social Media World

Contents

Foreword by Shannon Kaiser   xi
A Love Note from the Author   xvi

1:      Living in a Social Media World   1

PART ONE: PASSION
2:      Self-Love and Standards   13
3:      Authenticity and Alignment   21
4:      Inspiration and Intentionality   30
5:      Gratitude and Grace   39
6:      Empowerment and Evolution   44
Passion in Action   49
Passion on Social Media   49

PART TWO: PEACE
7:      Boundaries and Balance   53
8:      Energy and Environment   63
9:      Silence and Synchronicity   75
10:      Freedom and Forgiveness   81
Peace in Action   89
Peace on Social Media   90

PART THREE: POWER
11:      Accountability and Alchemy   93
12:      Priorities and Possibilities   100
13:      Courage and Confidence   108
14:      Expansion and Empowerment   119
Power in Action   133
Power on Social Media   133

PART FOUR: PROSPERITY

15:	Acceleration and Abundance	137
16:	Creating and Cultivating	141
17:	Income and Influence	150
18:	Safety and Serenity	155
Prosperity in Action		161
Prosperity on Social Media		161

PART FIVE: PANACHE

19:	Meaning and Magnetism	165
20:	Weird and Wonderful	168
21:	Style and Substance	172
22:	Fun and Fearlessness	175
Panache in Action		181
Panache on Social Media		181

Your Bliss Awaits   183

Acknowledgments   184
About the Author   185
Recommended Resources   186

Foreword

When was the last time you went onto social media and left the experience feeling even better, stronger, and more connected to yourself and life? Chances are, not recently.

We seem to be living in a heightened time of extreme contrasts, with new posts, memes, opinions, and news articles—most showing fear, agendas, doom, and gloom. But this is only one small fraction and sliver of the full picture.

Over the past several months, I found myself feeling hopeless, disgusted, and annoyed at the social platforms and what they've become. But then I remembered what my dear friend Sheri Fink often says: "Social media is a gift of worldwide connection and an inspirational tool." I reminded myself, "We always get what we focus on." I was focusing on the separations, the judgment, and the fear. But what about all the good that was happening online? What about all the amazing things unfolding in the world? I shifted my focus to see the global community, opportunities for connection, truth, joy, and chances for laughter. I quickly changed my focus and recommitted to using social media as a positive platform to help move us all forward into more love and light, both with my own posts and what I choose to engage with.

The reason I share this story is because social media is just a reflection of our collective approach to life, amplifying our innermost needs, desires, and wants. If we want to feel better, we must start by looking at what we've been giving our attention to.

In this book, *InstaGrateful: Finding Your Bliss in a Social Media World*, Sheri demonstrates that, just like with anything else, the intention we bring forward is what matters most. We can use social media as a way to shame and blame others, try to prove others wrong, and feel bad about ourselves, or we can use it as a profound platform for connection, support, joy, and unity.

This book isn't just about your relationship with social media and how to use it for good. It is a metaphor and road map for living a life of more joy, connection, authenticity, and appreciation. And it will show you how everything is connected.

As the best-selling author of the books *The Self-Love Experiment* and *Joy Seeker,* and an international empowerment coach and speaker, I've been teaching principles over the past decade on how to connect with your true self and live the life you are made for. I've built up a large social media community because I am committed to using my online presence as a place of positivity, inspiration, and light. I've seen firsthand the power of coming together and believing in ourselves and possibilities. We can all choose to be the light, even in what sometimes feels like a dark world. We all have this choice. And as I share in my coaching and books, "The more you, you show, the more your life will flow."

What we are all searching for in our endless scrolls is connection and value. What if we find more value in our everyday life, then bring this to the online world? What kind of life would we live if we all chose to give purpose to our passion and live with more joy? Well this is the life both Sheri and I are committed to leading and teaching. You have the power within you to be happier, healthier, and more fulfilled, and it starts with a commitment to self and owning your PASSION, PEACE, POWER, PROSPERITY, and PANACHE, as Sheri has laid out in this book.

The truer you are to yourself, the easier your life will be, which is why I am so happy that Sheri has written this guide. Now is the perfect time to apply these principles for finding bliss within, despite what is happening out in the world. She shows us how to be intentional and purpose-driven with our actions. Whether we are posting on social media, looking for our dream relationship, or changing careers, it's all connected. Because how you feel on the inside will manifest on the outside.

Sure, this may seem like a book about social media, but that is only the tip of the iceberg. This book is about authenticity, joy, meaning, and purpose. It's about living a life that feels real, honest, and good from the inside out. As you start to practice and live the steps presented in this book, you'll see how miraculous your life can be. Things that used to feel stressful float away. Old limitations and beliefs are transformed with the truth. You soon learn that you are magnificent and deserve your own love and attention. Your true self wants to be seen, heard, and revealed so you can truly play with the world.

Another mantra I share often is, "Your true soul group can't show up until you do." Not only is Sheri a person to bring into your circle, she honors this time and time again. From what I know about Sheri and her mission on this planet, she is here to help you align with your true self. This book you hold in your hands is the road map.

Several years ago, I met Sheri at a mutual friend's event, and we instantly clicked. She quickly became one of my favorite people because she walks her talk as a beacon of light. Over the years, I've seen her open up even more to the life she is destined to live, one full of self-love, joy, and appreciation—a mission-driven life. I've seen her step into her bliss, a life of fairy tales, wonder, and awe. From moving to her dream location in sunny California (where we meet for green juice) to meeting her prince charming in the most romantic way possible, to having a "unicorn" at their wedding, to creating an empire of books and teachings, and to becoming debt free, she shows us all how to live a life that aligns with our values and what is possible when we walk in gratitude and love. She is here to help you discover your bliss.

There are a lot of distractions and fear in the world, and when we give our attention to these outside forces, we lose sight of our true authentic power. But Sheri is on a mission to connect you back to your power so you can live in harmony and peace. We all deserve to live in bliss, and, reader, you are in for a treat. You'll walk away with a profound connection to the world at large, others, and your own true self. You may even grow your social media channels and align with your heart's deepest desires. This book is a joyful read as Sheri teaches the golden rule for happiness, appreciation, and gratitude. Enjoy this journey as you dive deeper into your own path of *InstaGrateful*.

-Shannon Kaiser
Best-selling author of *The Self-Love Experiment* and *Joy Seeker*
www.playwiththeworld.com
@ShannonKaiserWrites

PASSION · PEACE · POWER · PROSPERITY · PANACHE

InstaGrateful

FINDING YOUR BLISS IN A SOCIAL MEDIA WORLD

A Love Note from the Author

Hello, Beauty!

You are breathtaking, smart, talented, unique, important, and worthy of your wildest dreams coming true. You deserve the very best in life, and today is the special day when you embark on a life-changing journey to get it. I'm delighted to share this adventure with you.

For more than ten years, I've been on a journey of self-discovery. During that time, I've marinated in personal development and learned from some of the true masters. For years, I've collected shells in my metaphorical bucket until the bucket grew too heavy to carry. I've spent the past five years sorting through all of the shells and determining which ones work for me and are the true treasures, returning the rest back onto the beach for someone else to discover. As a result of my dedication to my own self-improvement, I've taken the strategies I've learned and combined them with my own approaches to create, and fully live, my dream life.

I wrote this book in response to the hundreds of messages and questions I received from friends and Fans wanting to know how I accomplish so much in a short period of time while having more fun than anyone else they know. To do so in our hyper-busy, highly distracted social media world is really a matter of learning techniques that enable you to connect with your authenticity, stay focused, strengthen your inner self, stand in your power, and be a beacon of light and love. This book will show you how I do it and how you can, too.

After witnessing the growth of social media from a fringe platform to an almost ubiquitous part of most people's lives, I wanted to remind myself and others that we're much more than our social media profiles. I hope to encourage people to focus on improving ourselves and our own lives so much that we realize that what's going on in social media isn't nearly as important as the positive difference we're making in the world.

It's weird writing a self-help book. It implies that I know it all, but believe me, I do not. It's like creating an instruction manual for life when I don't have life all figured out. My experience in raising myself out of humble childhood beginnings, navigating treacherous waters to discover true love, and building a career beyond my wildest dreams has led me to learn so much about cultivating bliss in this crazy and confusing age, and I just couldn't keep it bottled inside. I had to share it with you.

I'm deeply grateful that I can live my childhood dream of being an author, a teacher, a speaker, and a "mermaid" who helps people build their self-esteem. Doing it all with the love of my life, my husband Derek Taylor Kent, is the biggest dream come true of all. It's fun to see your dreams come to life, especially the really big, juicy ones. I am truly blessed, and I hope to use what I've been given to bless many, many others.

The most powerful lesson I've learned is that everything is possible. Hold your vision, feel what it will be like to live your dream, and keep working toward it. Small steps every day add up to giant leaps every year. I'm committed to making this my best year yet: full of love, fun, adventure, joy, and accomplishments that make a difference.

I chose the lotus flower as a symbol for this book because the lotus is regarded as a symbol of purity, enlightenment, self-regeneration, and rebirth in many different cultures. For me, it represents strength, perseverance, inner beauty, and possibility through adverse conditions. Even when its roots are submerged in the dirtiest waters, the lotus produces a beautiful flower. You and I are like the lotus. We are growing through the mud of life and about to bloom into our biggest, fullest, most expressive selves.

My hope is that the self-discoveries you make while reading this book enable you to:
- Create more passion, peace, power, prosperity, and panache in your life
- Realize that your life is much more than your social media feed
- Design an irresistible life you love that's aligned with your values

- Live your wildest dreams with enthusiasm, intention, and gratitude
- Appreciate the life you have while cultivating more of what you want
- Blossom into the magnificent person you're meant to become
- Inspire and empower others to transform their lives

I'm in constant evolution as I continue to try new ideas, patterns, and habits to up-level my own life. And now that I've found a formula that works for me, I'm ready to share it not only with my friends and Fans, but with people like you all around the world who are ready to burst forth and become the beautiful flowers you were born to be. So, if you want to make your life more magical than ever before, have more fun, feel more fulfilled, live your dreams, and possibly even leave a legacy, grab your metaphorical bucket and join me on this life-changing adventure!

I've organized *InstaGrateful* according to five key areas: Passion, Peace, Power, Prosperity, and Panache. Much like the petals on a lotus, each represents an aspect of life that when awakened, elevates our potential, and enhances our experience so that we can fully grow and blossom.

This is the book I wish I had years ago. Hopefully, the lessons I've learned will help you create a dream-come-true life, too!

XOXO,

Living in a Social Media World

By definition, social media is a network of platforms, websites, and applications that enable people to create, share, and comment on text, photo, and video content. In practice, social media has transformed the world in dramatic ways, creating a new landscape in which every aspect of our lives can be simplified, shared, and sold for attention. The majority of people spend multiple hours using social media platforms daily. Its influence is ubiquitous, changing the way we connect, learn, explore, keep in touch, and use our free time. It shapes our world and the way we see ourselves within it.

I genuinely enjoy social media most days. I didn't always feel that way. I was reluctant to jump into, or even dip my toe into, the social media swimming pool for a long time.

I think of my social media accounts as my own personal magazine where I get to create and curate only the content that I want to share and engage with. The type of magazine that I want to read showcases inspirational stories about people who are making a positive difference; features the best feel-good books, movies, TV shows, and music to make you laugh and fall in love with life; contains uplifting resources for personal empowerment; highlights fun restaurants and travel destinations with tips for your visit; profiles inspirational couples and families; includes thought-provoking and heartwarming articles; and provides a list of exciting upcoming events, products, and opportunities that are tailored for my interests. That's exactly what I choose to share on my social media accounts: all the things I love and want to tell my family, friends, and Fans about so that they can experience the magic as well.

When I feel overwhelmed, sometimes I'll go a few days without posting or logging in. I only post when I really want to, which I know is counter to what most social media gurus say to do. But for me, it's not about getting attention at certain hourly increments each day, it's about sharing the people, places, and things that bring me joy.

Social media is a gift of worldwide connection and an inspirational tool. It's fun to connect with people all over the world and to get inspired by the content others are sharing. I love seeing the fun vacations people are taking—it inspires new additions to my Adventure List. When I was single, I loved seeing happy couples posting about each other. It was aspirational for me. I would think that having a loving relationship was possible for me, too. It reminded me not to settle for less than what I really wanted. Today, loving couples still inspire me and make me grateful for my loving husband and the life we're creating together. Business owners inspire me with their entrepreneurial journeys and help me envision a bigger impact for my business as well.

Social media is like anything else. It can be the best or the worst influence on you depending on who you're following and how you're using it. For me, I only want to follow people I actually like, respect, and admire. If someone starts posting negativity or hatred, I unfollow them. It's as simple as changing the channel. I'm seeking positivity and inspiration. If someone isn't a match for that, I just keep moving.

The impact that social media has on our world is undeniable. We are so much more than our social media profiles, and it's important to always remember that, even when it doesn't feel like it. If we focus on improving ourselves and infusing our own lives with passion, power, peace, prosperity, and panache, we'll remember that what's going on in social media isn't nearly as important as the positive difference we're making in the world.

It All Began with a Little Rose

Next year will be the tenth birthday of my first children's book, *The Little Rose,* and planting the seeds that grew to become my company, Whimsical World. So many things have changed in my life since I decided to publish that book. It's astounding to think about everything that's changed since then. I'm so grateful that I decided to take leap after leap after leap that led me to where I am physically, mentally, emotionally, and spiritually today.

I remember feeling terrified, anxious, and unsure before and during each decision along the way. And yet, I survived the transitions after making the tough changes, and I'm thriving and continuing to grow today. Now, I write books that inspire, delight, and educate children while planting seeds of self-esteem and high achievement that can have lifelong benefits. I am so happy and grateful to be living my dream!

Before becoming an author and entrepreneur, I was a marketing professional working for big brands. I enjoyed my job but wasn't feeling passionate and excited about it. I crafted a plan to leave Corporate America, and I did it in July 2010. At the time, I wasn't sure exactly what I'd be doing, I just knew that I needed to create massive space for a change in my life.

Then, I attended Jack Canfield's Breakthrough to Success conference. Jack Canfield is *The New York Times* best-selling author of *The Success Principles* and best known as the co-creator of the wildly successful *Chicken Soup for the Soul* book series. I had read many of Jack's other professional development books and was delighted to learn directly from him at his conference. I came home full of new ideas and tools to enhance my life. I knew they would make a positive difference if I used them consistently.

Even though I'm very detail-oriented and motivated, I had difficulty integrating his teachings into my daily life. So, I created a journal that consolidated everything onto one page per day and made it easy for me to take action, measure progress, and celebrate successes. Once I created it, my friends said that other people would benefit from using this powerful tool, and so I published it as *Dreams Come True: Your Daily Journal for Maximum Success & Well-Being*. It was my first experience in self-publishing.

A few months later, I attended Jack's Advanced Breakthrough to Success conference. He generously gave me the opportunity to share my story with the attendees, and I sold out of my entire stock of journals.

One of the first people to buy the journal asked me what else I had written, and I reluctantly revealed that I had written a story about a little rose growing up in a bed of weeds who thinks that she's the weed among them. She learns to embrace her differences as gifts and appreciate herself for the beautiful rose that she is. The woman said that she got goose bumps and that I HAD to do something with the story because her grandchildren needed that message. That's when the light bulb went on for me, and I thought that "maybe this can be a children's book."

I was simultaneously tantalized and terrified by the idea of publishing a children's book. I had never done it before. I didn't even know anyone who had. But, I felt so compelled to do it that I took action daily to make it a reality. My passion for the story and its potential positive impact on kids really enabled me to go for it.

Sharing my writing was a very difficult thing for me. Up until then, I had only shared things that I had written that pertained to business and marketing. *The Little Rose* was very personal to me because it poured from my heart at a time when I was really struggling. The idea for the story of *The Little Rose* came to me while I was driving to work one day. Although I was doing a great job and being consistently promoted, I had an embarrassing secret … I was being bullied by a woman in my office.

I tried everything I could think of at the time to make it stop, but it kept getting worse. I focused on my job and did the best I could while trying to minimize the big emotions I felt about the situation. That day in the car, I felt so desperate. I was bawling because I didn't want to go to the office. I had given up the façade of knowing what to do. I just kept thinking "help me, I'll try anything." While drowning in tears and hopelessness, the story revealed itself to me as if divinely inspired. It was as if I wasn't even writing it in that moment. It felt as though it was writing through me from beyond. I scrambled to find any bits of paper in the car that I could capture it with. The only writing utensil I could find was a mini-golf pencil the length of my pinky finger! At stoplights on the way to work, I wrote down as much as I could. It was a beautiful and surreal experience.

When I got home that night, I typed up the story, printed it out, and put it in a drawer. I didn't let anyone read it. I learned a lot through my experience of being bullied and realized that everyone has the right to shine brightly. It's senseless to dim your light to blend in with the rest of the dim bulbs. It wasn't until after the Advanced Breakthrough to Success conference over a year after I wrote my little story that I unearthed it, read it again, and decided to share it with the world.

Initially, I was scared to tell my story. I worried what others would think of me. I've learned that the most important thing is to be your authentic self. Trust that others will get what they're meant to get from their interactions with you. By telling my story, I enable others to be brave and share theirs. And, I've found that almost everyone can relate to the experience. When I was honest about it, things really started happening for me and my book. I probably wouldn't be writing this book today if I had never had the courage to pull the story of *The Little Rose* out of the drawer.

Social Media Evolution

Social media is a very interesting phenomenon. When I was finishing college, I had a dream to create my own online magazine. I called it "Brunch!" and aspired to go out and do fun things, write engaging articles about my adventures, and publish them online. (This was before the major magazines were online and before I was aware of the existence of blogs.) I wanted to highlight the good in the world around me and to do it without inundating readers with ads.

Although I had been shy and fairly quiet up until that point in my life, I had a growing desire to express myself creatively and to allow my voice to be heard. I wanted to do it so badly that I read books, attended classes, and learned HTML and Dreamweaver while I was in grad school. I enjoyed it so much that I started doing web design for my university and even taught others how to build websites in smart classrooms. It wasn't as scary to speak in public because I had something valuable to say and felt passionate about helping others express themselves creatively.

Fast forward a few years and I realized that without ad revenue, my little online magazine was more of a hobby than a business. So I reluctantly accepted a job doing multimedia and web design. I was entrenched in the corporate world for a few years before social media entered my awareness.

I still remember when it happened. I was working on a travel website in the computer lab at the University of California, Irvine, sitting in the back row with at least 20 computers in front of me. I looked up for a moment and noticed that every seat was full and every computer (every single one!) was on the same website, a site called Facebook. I had never seen anything like it! The students appeared to be obsessed with checking Facebook. Seeing them log on day after day led me to the conclusion that whatever Facebook was must be a massive waste of time, and I quickly refocused on my project.

A few years later, I found myself taking another look at Facebook and other social media platforms as a way to reach potential customers for the company I worked for. Many clients asked me about advertising on those increasingly ubiquitous sites, and I reluctantly created an account for the company on Facebook and Twitter. At the time, you also had to create a personal profile in order to operate a professional business page. So, there I was on Facebook for the first time feeling awkward and vulnerable.

I didn't post much at first. I primarily focused on the company's Fan page. In my early days on social media, I hid behind the company name and logo, posting as the voice of the company without ever revealing whose voice it really was. It went okay, but I never really had the fun with it that everyone else seemed to be having. For me, it was a means to an end, just one more task on an already insanely long to-do list.

In the meantime, I started receiving friend requests—some from people I knew and liked, some from high-school acquaintances, some from colleagues, and some from complete strangers. It was overwhelming, and I didn't really know how to navigate the situation.

My perspective drastically changed when I left my corporate career and became a full-time author, speaker, and entrepreneur. Suddenly, social media became the best way for me to connect with people all over the world, to discover other entrepreneurs, and to get inspired.

I was still posting in the third person (talking about myself instead of speaking from my own perspective), but I posted more frequently and became more comfortable with the platform. Then, something unexpected happened. I got a new smart phone and attempted to post a silly picture of me wearing new glasses and sipping a pink milkshake to my personal Facebook profile but accidentally shared it on my public Facebook Fan page instead. I didn't realize the mistake at first. When I did, I was mortified. Up until then, I had maintained a strict separation between my personal, playful self and my professional, serious career on social media. What would people think of me if I were posting frivolous things on my professional page?

Turns out, they would think that I was just like them, except now they knew more of who I really was. That was scary at first. But reading through the comments on my accidental authentically playful post, I realized that it had been my most popular post so far. I thought about the public figures that I most admire and the people I love. I don't just want to see them when they're walking red carpets and winning awards. I love seeing the behind-the-scenes moments and knowing how much they love their dogs. It's sharing the personal side (within reason) that makes me feel connected to them and like I know them as a person. It was a huge aha moment for me.

I began thinking of Facebook as the online magazine I had always wanted. I could create and curate photos, quotes, events, and updates about things I cared about. I could share my thoughts and inspirations with people all over the world. I could follow and support other people's journeys and get inspired by their successes. Something I originally thought of as drudgery had become something that I looked forward to engaging with almost every day, both personally and professionally.

As a business owner, social media is my favorite way to engage with Fans beyond in-person events. I've become more confident using Facebook and other platforms. I'm a very visual person, so I'm really enjoying Instagram these days. Each platform serves its own purpose, and I've found ways to make posting more efficient over the years.

I enjoy reading others' posts and encouraging them. I curate my feed so that I only see things that aren't disturbing (e.g., I don't want to see political rants, complaining, blaming, extreme negativity, etc.). If someone starts posting things that aren't in alignment with me or my goals, I block them and move on with my day. I have no time for abusive people in my life in any way. I choose to engage with social media to be uplifted and to uplift others. Everything else could easily become an energetic distraction.

I'm proud of who I am, and it's worth taking the risk to show my authentic self in order to serve as a beacon for people who like my particular flavor of weirdness. If other people don't like it, that's okay. They can keep moving along their way. If I don't share my ideas, events, and excitements with the world, I will rob myself of the opportunity to connect heart-to-heart with people who appreciate my mission and my message.

In today's world, I feel like we need more positive role models and artists expressing themselves. Social media is a powerful way to reach people. The platforms are finding new ways to monetize every day, sometimes making it harder for us. However, you can still share your posts and people can discover you for free. (They might discover you faster if you pay for advertising on the platforms, but that's a discussion for another day.) Beyond the hype and the hyperbole, social media can be used as a powerful force for good.

That's why I felt it was important to write this book. Social media is often villainized in the media and blamed for many of society's ills. The problem with that pronouncement is that it completely negates personal choice and responsibility. We each have the power to decide what we will read, consume, and engage with. If we choose to hang out in "bad" neighborhoods, we shouldn't be surprised that bad things happen there.

We can take back our power to choose what is right for our unique selves and use these powerful tools to empower our lives, not to limit them.

We live in an exciting time in which we can do things that were unfathomable just 100 years ago. With electricity, the Internet, mobile devices, and the innovations that made them possible, we have so much possibility at our fingertips. It's astounding when you take a moment to consider all of the things we are personally capable of doing thanks to technology.

However, this tremendous blessing can also become a curse if we allow ourselves to be swept away into passively consuming the fruits of other people's labor (or the way they portray them on social media). It's natural to be curious about new things, but when we mindlessly wander from one shiny new thing to another, we may feel a momentary pleasure (like playing a slot machine) but pay the price long-term by not having the time to cultivate meaning in our own lives. Under the right circumstances, we're all susceptible to falling down the rabbit hole online. It's up to us to choose to make our work time and leisure time productive and worthwhile.

We each have 24 hours in a day. How are you going to use yours? Watching the news and scrolling on social media, or using technology as a powerful tool to accomplish your goals and live your dreams?

PASSION

Be thankful for what you have.
Be fearless for what you want.

When you strongly desire something and have astonishing energy around it, you have passion—the intense emotion that's behind ambition, courage, and persistence. I don't know about you, but when I'm passionate about something, I'm all in, turned on, ready to go, and enthusiastic about life. It's easy to walk through life trying to keep ourselves from getting too excited lest we end up being disappointed. But, life is much more fun and vibrant when you're revving up your passion and striving for a sense of more.

Passion is the excitement we feel about something we care about and the foundation for building the life of your dreams. Whether it's a friend, a lover, a child, a job, a skirt, a home, a promotion, a trip, a cause, etc., it's something that makes you happy to be alive. Typically, it's also something we can talk about in such a way that charms others into seeing the beauty or importance in it as well. If you've been going through the motions in your life and accepting whatever has been handed to you (been there, done with that!), you're going to be amazed at how your life transforms when you turn on your passion and go for what you really want.

Self-Love and Standards

Before we can bloom into the most beautiful expression of the lotus we're meant to be, it helps to focus on our point of attraction in the world: the way we love and care for ourselves.

Set Higher Standards to Live a Happier Life

Little daily choices can add up to lifelong consequences. Seemingly insignificant decisions, such as whether to work out one day or drink water instead of soda at lunch, when made regularly can result in healthy or unhealthy habits that put us on the path to our future. Making conscious choices and choosing the healthiest route will ultimately lead us to a brighter future, even when we don't want to see that truth in the moment. Self-discipline is a form of self-love.

We all know that we should drink water and get regular exercise, but how many of us have the mental, emotional, and physical self-discipline to follow through the majority of the time? It's so easy in our over-stimulated, always-on society to get wrapped up in doing things that are detrimental to our long-term well-being (and sometimes aren't good for the short-term, either).

Our on-demand world socializes us to desire instantaneous wish fulfillment. But that's not how the world really works. Anything that is truly meaningful and fulfilling happens over time with consistent effort. There is no quick-fix or five-minute solution for building a healthy body, a balanced lifestyle, or a successful business. These are endeavors that evolve and develop over years alongside the evolution of our character. Slow and steady still wins the race.

There's no need to beat ourselves up when we try something new and get less-than-stellar results. Part of growing up and living a good life is figuring out the unique formula for your own success and fulfillment. If you have a dream to do something, it can be done. But it won't be done by making other people responsible for your life.

Each of us has a unique responsibility to grow and create a life that we're excited to live. For me, that means aligning my actions with my values and my vision for my life. Do you know what's really important in your life? Do you know where you're going and have a plan to get there? Do you know how you want your life to feel? Once you have this treasure map, it's easier to see the value in self-discipline and healthy choices because it becomes clear which decisions move you closer to your goals and which ones do not.

If my goal is to write a book that empowers people worldwide to go for their dreams, and I choose to binge watch TV shows instead of making time to research and write, then I will never achieve the goal. Once you have a tantalizing vision for your future, the feelings associated with attaining that juicy vision will compel you to pursue it.

When you get started and see progress, you get even more amped up about the possibilities for your life. That's when momentum kicks in and you feel even more motivated to go for it. But, none of that happens until you choose a direction and start moving that way.

Once you start moving, you may be faced with decisions that require some soul searching. These choices are easier to make when you understand your top values. Values are like guideposts for your life. They help you remember what's most important and help to prioritize your actions and choices. My top values are:

1. Love and connection
2. Lifestyle freedom (business success and financial serenity)
3. Fitness and well-being
4. Fun, travel, and adventure
5. Contribution and legacy

Yours will probably be different from mine, but you can see how much easier it is to determine if an opportunity is right for me. I just measure it against this list and if it doesn't ring any of these bells, then it's not a fit for me. This is also helpful in planning my schedule. Each week, I want to be doing things that have a positive impact on each of these values. When my calendar and my actions are in alignment, I feel calm and confident, knowing that I'm making progress toward my goals and living a balanced and fulfilling life.

I'm finding, generally speaking, that the higher my standards, the happier my life. When I make choices that align with my highest values, I feel great and like I'm living my life to the fullest. When I deviate from them, I feel exhausted and unhappy, like something is off.

You can create this purpose, passion, and peace in your own life by determining your highest values and then mindfully choosing your activities. I like to use *The Passion Test* created by Janet Attwood and Chris Attwood. It's a simple, yet powerful tool for evaluating what you're most passionate about at the moment and can be used to assess your values, your priorities, and your goals to determine which make the biggest difference for you right now. *(See the Recommended Resources at the end of this book for details on where to discover more.)*

Don't Settle for Less than You Deserve in Life or in Love

When you love yourself and know what it feels like to be loved, you make different choices about who you get into relationships with. Secrets and lies are the currency of the desperate and the mediocre. Before I met Derek, I had dated my share of duds. They weren't all bad people, just not the right ones for me. It took valuing myself and my time, and realizing that I didn't want to settle for less than I really wanted, for me to stop dating just to date. Well-meaning friends would tell me that I "needed to get out there" and "just have fun." So, I tried online dating and was fixed up with countless dates that just didn't do it for me.

Everyone said that I should be having the time of my life, but for the most part, I didn't find dating to be fun or fulfilling. As a hopeful romantic, I was continually surprised and disappointed when my dating realities didn't match my romantic fantasies. There was the indecisive executive who geeked out on biohacking (the practice of changing our physiology through science and self-experimentation to energize the body) while hiding his heavy smoking habit, the selfish showbiz guy who was addicted to the spotlight and made me question my sanity, the rocket scientist who couldn't clear a real relationship for take-off, the kind engineer by day/salsa dancer by night who I didn't have chemistry with, the talented musician who turned out to love smoking pot even more than he loved music, the narcissistic entrepreneur who was faking it instead of making it, the enthusiastic younger man who turned out to be embarrassingly younger than I thought, the disenchanted drugstore executive who was bitter over his recent divorce, the acclaimed animator who flirted with me for a year but never got up the nerve to ask me out, the sushi-loving actor/director who wasn't sure what he wanted on the menu or in life, the older man who called himself my "big brother" before trying to manipulate me into being sexually involved with him, the hip hop-obsessed startup wunderkind who reminded me of a panda bear, the seemingly straight-laced writer who wanted to move way too fast, and numerous Peter Pans of all ages who refused to grow up and were looking for mothers instead of true partners. I had so many dates with men who were simply not "the one" that I felt disheartened. What can I say? You encounter a lot of characters when you live in a city like Los Angeles. It was difficult not to lose hope that true love existed.

I also met so many women who were having similar experiences or who had resigned themselves to relationships with men that they weren't really attracted to or happy with, just for the "safety" of being with someone. I wanted something real with someone who was real. And I wasn't willing to waste any more time or energy with men who showed early signs that they weren't "the one." I'm embarrassed to share that it took me years to come to this conclusion.

The frustration and lonely feelings I experienced during that time fed part of the inspiration for my romance novel, *Cake in Bed.* I don't want to settle for feeling "safe-ish" in my relationship or in my life. I want to be with a man who shares that ambition to feel passionate and alive and who is willing to do the work so that, together, we can create the life we want to live. I'm very blessed that my dream has come true. But it didn't happen by accident. It took saying "no" to the wrong guys so that I was available physically, mentally, emotionally, and spiritually to say "yes" to the right guy when he came along.

Be the Bird

When I was going through my awkward dating period, a wise friend of mine told me about the bowerbird. This female bird is well known for demanding a beautiful nest before she will choose a mate. The male bowerbirds gather everything they can to build a special home to impress the female. Some use flower petals, others use bottle caps, many use berries, sticks, and seeds. If the female bird flies over and isn't impressed with his architecture or decorations, she flies away without even giving a second look.

My friend would remind me to "be the bird" when I found myself dating men who weren't the right fit for me and was making excuses for them. His point was well taken. It was a playful reminder not to settle for a person or a situation that isn't the best one for me. There are so many people in this big world of ours. If you haven't met your bird of choice (the one who treats you the way you deserve to be treated) yet, don't waste time trying to make it work. Just be kind and fly away. You'll save yourself time and heartache. The right bird for you could be building your love nest around the corner. You'll never know unless you keep your options open until you find the right one.

Extraordinary Self-Care

It's embarrassing to admit, but there was a time in my life when I was in college that I had a hard time taking a daily vitamin consistently. Even though I was always a goal-driven, hard-working person, I didn't value taking care of myself. Everything else felt more important and, if I had extra time after getting everything else done, I would tell myself that then I would do my personal things. I feel sad when I look back on that time in my life where I was my last priority.

If you can relate, know that I've been there, came through it, and so can you. It starts with small steps, such as taking your vitamins each day. As you continue taking those steps, you build up your consistency muscles and can begin enhancing your self-care, which will up-level your life. Most people I meet have a burning desire to help other people. But, you can't help people at the level you want to when you're not making the time to take care of yourself.

Self-care is not selfish. It's one of the greatest gifts you can give to yourself and the world. When you feel strong, confident, wealthy, rested, and joyful, you can be generous with your gifts to others on a whole new level. As Lisa Nichols says, "your job is to fill your own cup so it overflows. Then you can serve others, joyfully, from your saucer."

There's another magical thing that happens when you take extraordinary care of yourself inside and out—you feel happy and fulfilled. When your needs are met, you don't look to the outside world to meet them for you. When you feel like a beautiful goddess who's in love with life, you show up differently in your daily life and you make better decisions than someone who feels like a schlub.

I know when I have my hair and make-up done professionally, I feel like I'm walking down the street in one of those shampoo commercials—hair flowing, smile glowing, people knocking each other down to open doors for me. Don't you feel that way? What if we each walked out of our front door every day with that level of passion, joy, and confidence? What magic would you attract if you did? What would it take for you to create that sensation in your life?

One of the things I started doing as a self-care activity was my nails. I didn't think it was that important until I started appearing on camera in interviews. I subconsciously would hold my hands down because I didn't think they looked as feminine and professional as I thought they could. When I got my nails done, I had a new level of confidence on camera and my gestures became more organically authentic. I have a lot going on with my life and business and don't always make time to visit the nail salon these days. Instead, I do at-home mani-pedis using stick-on nail polish in fun colors that include lots of sparkle. It saves me time and money and still gives me the look I love.

Let's brainstorm ways to take care of ourselves and make a list of self-care activities that you want to try. You don't have to commit to doing everything you choose every day, just acknowledge the ideas that intrigue you for now. If you find yourself hovering over an idea unsure of whether or not to check the box, check it. Here are a few ideas to get your creative juices flowing:

Bubble bath	Nap	Spa day
Salt-soak bath	Swim	Vision boarding
Meditation	Gardening	Adventure day
Journaling	Vacation	Stay-cation
Praying	Painting	Yoga
Massage	Workout	Dance
Manicure	Pedicure	Facial
Flower arranging	Cooking	Baking
Drawing	Writing	Coloring

Whatever it is that tickles your fancy, write it down. These are ideas to help you look and feel your best, to fully embody the goddess that you already are.

Authenticity and Alignment

Magic becomes a common occurrence in our lives when we align our actions with our values and our authentic selves. Doing so helps make us a magnet to attract what we really want. We can accelerate our growth and enhance our happiness by discovering who we are and staying true to ourselves.

Authenticity Is Key

I'm allergic to inauthenticity and entitlement. There's just something you can sense about someone who thinks they're superior to others or deserves something for nothing. I can't always articulate it, but that funny feeling inside me has never been wrong.

People may think they can do what someone else does and get the same results, but they really can't. They see the final product, but they have no idea how much goes into every element behind the scenes. It's like seeing a piece of cake and attempting to replicate the look of it, except the original cake is full of delicious ingredients and made with love and careful planning. The imitation cake is pretty icing on a piece of Styrofoam that's cut to look like a cake. They can't fool people for long—and they can never really fool themselves.

Let's focus on being the real deal, the delicious and gorgeous cake, instead of the Styrofoam imitation. Who would you be if you could be anyone? What would you do with your day if your time was completely free and you had unlimited resources? Who do you most like to spend time with? What activities uplift you and remind you what you're capable of? We can take it another level by creating a "Love List" of everything you love and appreciate about yourself. Now is not the time to be modest. Take a few minutes to write down everything that's great about you.

These are all clues as to who you really are. The positive feelings you experience when you're considering these authentic joys and wishes will serve as guideposts along this journey.

Working on a Dream Home

When I was in high school, my mom fell in love with a fixer-upper of a house. It was halfway completed, and she was dating someone who was in the construction industry. He claimed that he would help finish building the house, so my mom made the leap and purchased her dream home.

When we moved in, we all assumed that the home would be finished quickly. We now know that's not how construction projects generally go. Within the first year, everything that could go wrong did. They weren't able to focus on finishing the house because they had to fix things that had already been built improperly, deal with leaking skylights, and repair damage that had been hidden during the buying process. For years, I resented that all of our family's money was being poured into a house that didn't show meaningful improvements for a long time.

To top it all off, my mom's office in our local area was closing, and now she had to commute two hours each way to work in another city to keep earning the salary she needed in order to continue paying for the house. My mom was beyond stressed, and my sister and I didn't make it any better. As time went on with the house unfinished, I felt embarrassed that we had drywall everywhere and didn't have a proper living room/family room. I was resentful that I had to take on more responsibility and that we wouldn't eat dinner until 8–9 p.m. when my mom got home from work. It seems so silly now, but back then the sight of building supplies all over the house used to make me bitter. Although I liked the house and thought it would be beautiful when it was finished, I didn't think that it was really worth all of the sacrifices we were making.

It wasn't until years later (once the relationship ended) that my mom finally got her dream home through hard work, persistence, and an unstoppable will. My mom is one of the strongest people I've ever known. She didn't have a background in construction, home design, or carpentry, but took it upon herself to research how to do everything that needed to be done (or hire qualified people to do it) in order to turn the unfinished property into the home of her dreams. Year after year, she has systematically taken on new home projects and impressed me with her results. The house is now finished and functional. Every detail is perfectly suited for her and her tastes. She even assembled all of the furniture herself! She's amazing.

I remember sitting in my backyard in California during one of her visits and she confessed to me that maybe buying the house when she did wasn't the best idea and that holding onto it once her job circumstances changed was also a bad choice. I was really taken aback. For years, I wanted her to acknowledge that she had made a mistake in taking on that property and sacrificing the time with us in order to keep it. But sitting in the sunlight on that warm day, I looked at her and saw the situation much differently.

Owning that house was my mom's big dream. She grew up disadvantaged with a hard-working mother and step-father but no car or indoor plumbing. She graduated from high school at a time when women rarely did and was the first person in our family to have a white-collar job. She took two years off from work to be with me when I was a baby and went back to work quickly after my sister was born. Here was a woman who worked her whole life to finally own something of quality. I finally saw that the house represented the American dream to her, and she deserved it.

As someone who's relentlessly pursued my dreams from an early age, sometimes to the chagrin of my family and friends, I could finally relate to my mom on a new level. Instead of agreeing with her that it had been a miscalculated choice, I found myself reinforcing her decision to take a chance on the house and on love. She didn't know at the time that the relationship wasn't going to work out. She hoped for the best and went for it. Isn't that what we all do when we're really going for our dreams?

For the first time, I saw my mom for the bold trailblazer and risk-taker that she is. I realized that we are more alike than I had thought and that maybe my spunky spirit comes from her. It was my honor to reassure my mom that she made the best choices she could in those moments and that now she has a beautiful home that she worked for and fully deserves.

Even though pursuing her dream was tough for many years, she did it anyway and modeled that relentlessness for us. I admire her and applaud her for doing whatever it took to make her dream come true. I'm very proud of her and her accomplishments. It makes me happy when I think about her enjoying her handiwork in her very special home.

It Had to Be You

Several years ago, I was invited to speak at an elementary school as part of an Author Festival. My friend, a fellow children's book author, was organizing the event and gathered 20 authors from the Los Angeles area to speak at his children's school. I was honored to be a part of it and had no idea that saying "yes" to that opportunity to inspire kids to love reading and writing was about to change my life forever.

It started like any other author event with meet and greets with the other authors, going to our respective classrooms to speak, returning for lunch in the library with the teachers and staff, and then speaking again before our book signing that afternoon. During one of the behind-the-scenes breaks between presentations, I met Derek. He was sitting across a big, round table from me as I said hello and introduced myself to everyone at the table. I had heard of his ultra-successful *Scary School* book series and recognized him even though we had never met in person.

We had a brief conversation about speaking at schools, and he introduced me to the wonders of coconut water for saving your voice. I saved him from a wardrobe malfunction, which made us both crack up laughing. It was a pleasant exchange that led to him friending me on Facebook. I'm blessed to meet a lot of great people and have fun conversations every day, so I didn't think much else of it. He would message me every now and then sharing a strategy that worked for him and encouraging me to check it out.

Several months later, I was attending Comic-Con International in San Diego and had just finished my morning workout when I received a message from Derek asking if I wanted to meet up at Comic-Con. I rarely make commitments to meet with people during that crazy week. Lines can be long for things I want to attend, and I never know exactly how much time I'll have between engagements. So, I graciously declined his invitation and went about getting ready for the day. I rode the bus to the Convention Center, walked through a Superman vs. Batman exhibit, took photos for a family, and then was approached by a kid who yelled out, "Hey, I know you! You're famous." Blushing, I asked if I had spoken at his school. He confirmed it and asked for a photo and an autograph. I was happy to oblige. Then, I turned around to walk toward the Convention Center and ran into Derek!

In a sea of thousands in the Gaslamp Quarter, I literally bumped right into him while he was handing out mini posters promoting his book, *Kubrick's Game*. I couldn't believe it! Of course, synchronicities happen for me all the time, so I shouldn't have been so surprised. I told him I was thinking about getting lunch, and he said he'd love to have lunch together but there's no way we'd be able to get into any of the restaurants because they were so busy. I said not to worry, that I have great luck. So, he pointed to a place and said that he'd meet me there after he handed out the rest of his posters.

I walked in and, despite their busyness, was able to get us a place at the bar. He came in a few minutes later in disbelief that I was able to get seated so quickly. I simply smiled. Lunch was professional and friendly, but not flirty. He seemed to know who I was and was very respectful of the business I'd built. He wasn't asking for help with anything, which was what typically happened when dining with another author. As a matter of fact, he was thinking of things that might help me with my books (but not in a critical way). After we paid for our lunches, we walked toward the Convention Center together and he told me about the fun experiences and activities that were set up outside. He walked with me for a bit as I checked them out before he left to attend a panel.

I remember thinking that this lunch and interaction had been very different from any that I had before. I was dating at the time, and I felt like this lunch was better than any date I'd ever been on, even though it wasn't a date. I remember telling my mom about it afterward, and she said, "Well, maybe that's the kind of masculine energy you need in your life." I didn't think much more about it, just went on my way enjoying my adventures in "Nerdvana."

A few months later, I was throwing an after-party following a children's book festival, and I invited Derek along with a long list of author and illustrator friends who I knew would be attending the event. I was tired of working all day at the festival, not getting to talk to my friends even though they were also there, and then going to dinner by myself. I figured that it would be awesome to gather a group of friends at a local restaurant after the event so we could eat, catch up, and relax before we all drove home.

At the festival that day, Derek stopped by my booth to say "hello" and, to my surprise, showed up during my reading on stage (even though it was during his book signing). I saw him standing there in the back, taking pictures, and clapping for me. I was impressed that he took the time away from his own booth to see me perform and then helped me carry my books back to my booth.

That night, he was waiting in the bar at the restaurant and had ordered a virgin piña colada (one of my favorites as I absolutely cannot handle any hard liquor). When we were seated at the long span of tables, I sat in the middle, and he sat right next to me, even though that meant that no one would be able to sit in the rest of that side because we were blocking them. We decided to move down to the end when other friends arrived to make room for everyone. He was kind, funny, humble, and awkwardly charming. I was amazed that he remembered that I'm pescatarian, from our lunch months before. By the end of dinner, I was having a fabulous time and was completely recharged from the long day. (I'm typically exhausted at the end of those events.) I gave each of my friends a hug and said good night. I remember thinking that I wish I could spend more time with him.

The next day he asked me out, and we've been together ever since. I knew after a month of dating that he was the one for me. There was just something so different about him and about the way he treated me. He respects and cherishes me like no one has before. He's brave, honest, and makes me laugh every day. I had been looking for the one for years, and I had hoped that my soulmate would understand me and appreciate my business. Not only does Derek have a deep understanding of what it takes to be a successful author and entrepreneur, he is living it himself. He's secure in his masculinity and loves to see me shine.

It's incredible to be able to share that passion and so many others together. I'm not sure many spouses would like the schedule that comes along with being a creative entrepreneur: up early on weekdays to speak at schools, working at night to write new books, and traveling most weekends to do events, book signings, and keynotes. We get to do all of these things together, which is the absolute best-case scenario.

I remember when we were dating, and he casually mentioned that he had a costume closet. I had never heard of such a thing. (It's a closet that's dedicated to storing costumes.) My husband was in theater and had costumes from his musicals and shows. As someone who has always loved to dress up and who does cosplay, this sparked my interest. I had costumes that needed a closet. How perfect was that? I always tell people that if there was a man put on this planet that was made perfectly for me, then anything is truly possible. Your miracle could be just around the corner.

Trust Your Instincts

The day my husband proposed to me was a magical day. He surprised me during dinner at home, and when he popped the question, it was the biggest full-body sensation of "yes" that I had ever felt. I didn't have to think about, analyze, or consider any alternatives. I just knew deep down inside that he was the one and that we were meant to be together.

In contrast, there had been decisions I had made in my life before that had left me feeling unsure, disconnected, and even panicked. I've discovered through trial and error that the best decisions are the ones I make when my body feels like "YES!" The worst ones are when my body starts to ache or my mind feels foggy. If I feel instantly tired, that's usually a bad sign.

I've learned to trust these instincts even when they don't seem to make sense. Once, I was hiring a personal trainer and was interviewing three possible candidates. I liked each of them, but there was one who when I looked at him, the vision in my left eye went blurry and sometimes looked blank (I couldn't see anything). It was a strange sensation, but it continued throughout our conversation to the point where I couldn't ignore it. Even though he was the lowest-priced option and seemed like a "nice guy," I chose someone else because I trusted that my body was trying to tell me that he wasn't the best choice for me. I still don't know or worry about the reason. It really doesn't matter. I got the message my body was sending and chose differently. Of course, I didn't tell him that's why I went with someone else. You don't owe anyone an explanation for following your instincts. Just trust them and let them guide you down the right path for you.

Follow the Yellow Brick Road

I'm finding more and more that the seemingly disparate jobs I've had over the years have led me to who I am and what I'm doing today. I learned about marketing, negotiating, leading, managing, partnering, and planning from my years in the corporate world. I learned about speaking and teaching while leading tech classes in smart classrooms while I was in grad school. I learned about customer service while working as a receptionist at a woman-owned real estate company. I learned about sales and merchandising from working in retail stores. Every one of the roles helped me develop knowledge, skills, and experience that makes me a better entrepreneur.

The same is true for my husband who was a theater major, did improv comedy, wrote and directed musicals, acted, and worked for a talent agent. He's using all of those skills to write books, screenplays, and articles; to make kids laugh; to communicate with business partners; and to perform on stage with me. I bet if you look back on your work life, you'll find that you've grown and evolved from your various jobs as well.

PASSION

I learn so much every day as an entrepreneur. I feel like being in business has supercharged my personal evolution. It's helped me to prioritize my time and values better, to become a better steward of my finances, to improve my communication and negotiation skills, to connect better with my Fans, and of course, to improve my writing skills. I find that when I'm aligned with my pure intention, it gets easier as I become a magnet for what I want to attract. Each day is an exciting adventure as I do my best and allow the magic to unfold.

Inspiration and Intentionality

Aligning our intentions with our inspiration empowers us to go for our dreams and to stay on the path when the journey gets bumpy. Joy is an experience we can cultivate and nurture in our daily lives. Sharing joy with others is a worthy intention that will keep us inspired along the way.

Vacation Vibes

What is it that we love so much about going on vacation? For me, it's the attention to details that we put into planning our meals and plotting our adventures; the savoring of the moments with loved ones because we know this is a special time; the presence we have as our minds are free from work matters to focus on the art of living; the indulgences of sleeping in, spending money, and enjoying desserts; the awareness that we're actively creating memories that matter; the giving of our time and attention to our loved ones and receiving them in return; and taking the time to breathe and relax beyond our routines.

What if we could set up our lives to enable us to experience these feelings on a daily (or at least weekly) basis? What would it take to create the environment for these feelings to be natural by-products of our regular lives?

Appreciate Small Moments

I love nature and animals. My husband bought me a hummingbird feeder and special hanger that enables it to defy gravity and dangle right outside my second-floor office window. Colorful hummingbirds visit throughout the day and make me smile noticing their beauty, the incredible details of nature, and reminding me that my husband enabled those joyful moments especially for me.

Instagrateful

I hope you enjoy your book.
If so, I would be honored if you'd take
a moment to write a review on Amazon.
Wishing you bliss!

With love and gratitude,

It means even more knowing that the first three feeders and holders didn't work. The hanger would detach and the feeder would fall into the yard below and burst open. I felt sad seeing those busted feeders and knowing that the hungry little birds wouldn't be visiting my window anymore. My husband was determined. He researched the best equipment, adhesives, feeders, and nectar, and we've been feeding delightful little hummingbirds ever since, which fills me with gratitude

create joy in small moments throughout your

lives? One technique I learned from Jack Canfield is to create a Joy List. List out 20 things that you love to do. It can be anything you enjoy: baking cupcakes, taking a walk, calling a friend, making love to your spouse, journaling, going on vacation, reading, dancing, skydiving, etc. Just write 20 activities that make you feel happy to be alive. Then, next to each activity, write the approximate last time you did it (or the frequency that you do it, e.g., weekly).

If you're like me, you may feel saddened by how rarely you currently do these fun things. Don't feel bad. We all get swept up in busyness and taking care of others from time to time. But now's the time to focus on taking care of yourself. Go through your list and choose one activity you can do this week to bring more joy and liveliness into your life.

Then, schedule some of these activities on your calendar for the coming months. The goal is to do at least one thing you love from your Joy List once a week. I noticed an immediate boost in my energy and happiness when I began practicing this in my own life. I was even hired once to mentor a woman to help her have more fun. That was an incredible job! We started with her Joy List, and she gradually began feeling more alive, trusting herself and her authentic desires, and enjoying her life on a deeper level.

Never Underestimate Your Impact

When I was a little girl growing up in rural Virginia, I didn't have many friends. My first friend was my babysitter, a woman who was in her late 50s that had run away from home as a teenager and never learned to drive a car. She lived one street over from mine, and my parents hired her to take care of me and my sister in her home while they were at work.

Although she never had a traditional job outside of her home, Patsy was one of the hardest working people I had ever known. Every day, she would clean her entire house from top to bottom. Every day!!! She always cooked us a big lunch and then we'd nap while she watched her "stories" (soap operas). I spent more time with Patsy than I did with my own parents back then.

Patsy listened to me. Not how an adult typically listens to a child in a half-listening kind of way and then pats them on the head undervaluing what was said because it came from the mouth of a child. She actually listened to me, my thoughts, my dreams, my fears. She didn't patronize me or treat me like a child. I felt genuinely seen and loved by this special lady.

One of the things Patsy loved to do was to play word games. She would write a phrase (e.g., Happy Birthday) at the top of three sheets of paper. She would then sit with us at the kitchen table and give my sister and me each a paper. She would keep the third one for herself. We would all write as many words that we could come up with made from the letters in the phrase. Once we ran out of ideas, we would all count our words and she would award a little prize to the winner. In the beginning, she would win almost every time. But over the years, Julie and I got better and better until we began winning consistently. I still have those prizes (often little Christmas ornaments from Avon) and cherish them.

Patsy was definitely not a wealthy woman, but she made a deal with Julie and me. For every "A" we brought home on our report cards, she would give us a quarter. Julie and I always worked hard and did well in school, and this was added incentive to do our very best. Patsy was so proud of our achievements and beamed as she awarded the quarters to us. It made us feel important to have an adult cheering us on.

One year, I asked for Boggle for Christmas. I was thrilled when Santa brought it and I could play word games all the time. The only problem is that I couldn't find anyone who was available and willing to play with me. By that time, I was old enough to stay home by myself and to watch over my little sister. But that didn't stop me from riding my bike over to Patsy's house and playing Boggle with her. She wasn't even being paid to watch me. She hung out with me because she cared about me and wanted to play the game. That meant so much to me as a kid. I knew that I had a safe place to go no matter what.

I suspect that Patsy planted a seed within me to love words. And now, all these years later, I find myself writing books that help kids embrace their authentic selves and go for their dreams—just like Patsy has always encouraged me to do.

Now that I live in California, I don't get to see her that often. Whenever I'm back in Virginia, I try to stop by for a visit. For a few years, my timing was off, and she would be away while I was in town. Thankfully, I was able to visit her this Christmas along with my mom, sister, nephew, and husband. I was grateful to spend time with her and introduce her to Derek. While we were there, she pulled out the stack of books that I've sent her over the years, along with a stack of cards and letters I wrote to her that she'd kept. It really touched me that she'd held onto them and that they meant something to her, and that I still mean something to her.

My mom taught me to read before I went to kindergarten, so those seeds had already been planted from an early age, but I don't know for sure that I would've been as interested in words, writing, and doing well in school if it hadn't been for Patsy nurturing those seeds within me. Every time I see Patsy, I'm reminded of how much she means to me and the difference she's made in my life.

Never underestimate the impact you can have on someone's life. Everyone has the opportunity to show up and be fully present for another at some point in their lives. Patsy didn't have to spend time with me. She was being paid to let me play in her house and keep me out of trouble. But she took it to the next level and not only spent time with me, but also made me feel important and, ultimately, became my dearest friend. I hope that one day I can have that impact on a child, just like Patsy had on me.

Unicorn Lovers Unite

One of my favorite books as a young child was *Leo the Lop* by Stephen Cosgrove. He is most well-known for his unicorn book, *Morgan and Me*. I didn't know it at the time, but Cosgrove had built Serendipity Press, an independent publishing empire of over 300 books, before anyone knew what self-publishing even was. A few years ago, Derek and I were traveling back from appearances in the Bay Area and stopped at a restaurant on the way home. They had an elaborate gift shop and while we were browsing, I came across an entire section of books by Stephen Cosgrove.

I was delighted to discover *Leo the Lop* hiding in the rack and purchased it. I told the clerk my story about loving his books as a kid, and she said that he's a very nice man who delivered the books himself. I was intrigued by that and decided to write him an email of appreciation (fan letter) when I got home. To my surprise, he wrote a lovely and encouraging note back to me less than five minutes later! I was so happy about it that I posted it on my Fan page, and one of my friends direct messaged me that he's her dad! What a small world.

Fast forward a year or so later, and I find out that there's an annual Unicorn Festival in Colorado. It's a two-day, outdoor event in which people come together to celebrate everything magical, including fairies, mermaids, dragons, and unicorns. Guess who the guest of honor was? None other than the amazing Stephen Cosgrove! I wanted to attend so badly, but already had author events booked for that weekend. Luckily for me, the dates the following year worked, and I traveled to Denver to headline the Unicorn Festival, just like one of my heroes did the year before. I just received word a few weeks ago that Stephen Cosgrove and I will be co-headlining the next Unicorn Festival, and I couldn't be more excited. I'm deeply honored and can't wait to meet him in person. His books played an important role in my personal development as a child, and I hope that my books will continue to help kids in the same way. It's going to be a very special weekend.

Creative Inspiration: The Story Behind the Story

Inspiration is everywhere when you're open to finding it—or allowing it to find you. People often ask me where I get the ideas for my books. I'm most often inspired by real-life experiences and emotions. Here's the inside scoop behind each of my books so far:

The Little Rose – The story of a little rose who grows up in a weed bed and, because she's different, thinks that she's the weed. She discovers that she's a beautiful rose no matter what anyone else says and find friends who appreciate her for who she really is. I was inspired to write this book after experiencing bullying myself and wanting to empower children to build their self-esteem so that they would be unshakable by anyone else's opinions of them.

The Little Gnome – The Little Gnome arrives in the garden in the summer and loves it. But when things start to change, he doesn't understand or like the changes at first. He learns to look for the good in every season and situation. For this story, I thought about what it would be like if a child from California was taken to live in a place like Virginia and no one had told him about the four seasons. I wanted to help kids become more optimistic and adaptable to change. Moving to California was an enormous change for me, and I could only imagine what it would be like for a child. While kids crave stability, it's important to learn that change is a natural part of life.

The Little Firefly – The Little Firefly is the last one to glow and fakes it in hilarious ways so she can play a sport called "Fire Tag" with her friends. When they find out, she learns what real friendship is about. I've always loved fireflies and was surprised that California did not have them. I enjoyed their magical twinkling lights throughout the summers of my childhood and wanted children to know what they are regardless of where they live. I also have a younger sister who was almost the same size as me growing up but who wasn't old enough to participate in the same activities. I thought about what that must've felt like and wrote it from her perspective.

The Little Seahorse – The bashful Little Seahorse has to learn to speak up, ask for help, and make new friends in order to bring a gift home for his mom. I was very shy as a kid (and sometimes as an adult), and I felt like I missed out on a lot of opportunities and friendships as a result. I wanted to empower kids to be brave and to ask for what they want help with.

The Little Unicorn – The Little Unicorn loses her sparkle (the worst thing that can happen to a unicorn) and goes on a journey far away to find it, only to discover it's always within her. I've always loved unicorns, and I was inspired to write this book to encourage kids to look within themselves for confidence and validation, not to the external world. When we believe in ourselves and support our friends, the world is a much more magical place.

The Little Dragon – The Little Dragon loves to dance in his meadow. One day he's overwhelmed with emotions when someone giggles at him. He learns to express big feelings (fear, anxiety, embarrassment, and anger) in a healthy way and to make a new friend. I wanted to write a book that would help kids recognize and deal with overwhelming emotions and be brave enough to dance. My dad has never been a confident dancer, but I was able to convince him to dance with me at my wedding celebration in Virginia. Those moments are a precious reminder to dance when the opportunity presents itself.

Exploring the Garden with the Little Rose – This is an alphabet book featuring the Little Rose that takes young kids on an adventure learning the upper- and lower-case letters and garden vocabulary. As someone who has always loved flowers and words, it was fun to teach kids to love them, too.

Counting Sea Life with the Little Seahorse – An interactive underwater adventure that teaches kids to count 1–30 while learning about sea animals and finding hidden numbers. This was my first collaboration with my husband and was inspired by the proliferation of STEM learning. We wanted to find a way to make counting fun for toddlers.

World of Whimsy with the Little Unicorn – A baby board book that introduces whimsical creatures, including unicorns, mermaids, fairies, dragons, and Pegasus. The most magical one of all is at the very end—a mirror reflecting the baby reading the book! I was inspired to write this book to read with our future baby.

Cake in Bed – A fun and flirty romance novel about a 30-something divorcee finding real love after multiple missteps. It's a smart and sexy happily ever after story for the modern, yet old-fashioned woman. Writing this book came as a surprise to me and was one of the most fun books to write. I wanted a romance novel that was something I actually enjoyed reading. I couldn't find one so I decided to write it myself.

My Bliss Book: An Inspirational Journal for Daily Dream Building and Extraordinary Living – A daily journal that helps align your schedule with your values and goals, keeps you accountable, and enables you to create more magic, passion, and happiness in your life. I was practicing these behaviors daily and decided to make my formula available for others to enjoy and excel as well.

InstaGrateful: Finding Your Bliss in a Social Media World – An inspirational self-help book that empowers readers to realize that you're much more than your social media profile. I wanted to encourage people to focus on improving themselves and their own lives and realize that what's going on in social media isn't nearly as important as the positive difference they're making in the world.

I'm proud of all of my books because they poured from my heart. I've written in multiple genres and the common thread is that my books are about self-love and are designed to be uplifting and to empower readers to believe in themselves. I'm not exactly sure what I'll write next. We'll see where the inspiration takes me!

Gratitude and Grace

Studies have shown that gratitude is one of the strongest positive emotions we can feel. It's important to practice gratitude for what we have now as we reach for what we want in the future. When we feel grateful, we're in a better position to be compassionate, loving, and understanding (all forms of generosity). This leads to higher-quality relationships and more fulfilling lives.

Give People Grace

What's more important: the way my loved one feels or what someone else thinks? Sometimes, it's easy to be impatient with someone or to believe, and even declare, that our way of doing things is better. But most of the time, it doesn't really matter. What's more important is allowing people to be who they are and giving them the grace to do it their way, even if it's not the way we would do it.

Giving people grace enables them to relax in our presence instead of walking on eggshells and trying to be perfect around us. Let people be who they are and make mistakes. There's no need to be a know-it-all that makes everyone feel like they're below you. If someone asks for your advice, willingly share. But if they don't request your guidance (and it's not a life-or-death situation), then lead by example. What we do, and how we live, teaches people far better than our judgments and advice ever could.

It's important to extend this grace to ourselves as well. It's okay to try new things, to not know the answer, and to make mistakes. None of us are perfect and so we shouldn't hold ourselves to an impossible standard. High standards and healthy boundaries are good, perfectionism is not.

The Language of Love

While attending one of Jack Canfield's Breakthrough to Success conferences, I was introduced to the Five Love Languages that were created by Gary Chapman. Gary theorizes that there are five primary ways that people like to give and receive love and affection.

After the conference, I purchased the book, took the assessment inside, and began marveling at how it helped me understand myself and others better. Based on a series of responses to questions, Gary helps you rank the order of preference of your top love languages. Understanding how you most like to receive love can help you talk with your loved ones about what you need. It also gives you a way to talk with them about how you can help them feel more loved.

The biggest aha moment I had was that my mom's primary love language is Gifts. In contrast, Gifts is low on my list. My mom always puts so much thought and time into shopping for the gifts she gives. It's like a work of art opening presents from her on Christmas morning. Every gift is carefully considered, high quality, and impeccably wrapped. When I was younger, I wanted to give her the ability to choose whatever she wanted since she loved to shop so much. I was afraid of choosing something that was not perfect for her. So, one year I gave her gift cards to her favorite stores. She was grateful but seemed a little disappointed, and I didn't understand why until I read Gary's book.

Because my mom's primary love language is Gifts, she feels most loved when people invest the time, research, and care into finding the right gift for her. When I gave her the gift cards, she didn't feel as loved because it didn't seem as if I had invested any time in finding the gift. This realization helped me to understand that I needed to spend more time brainstorming and choosing the right gifts, not just for her, but for everyone. I'm happy to say that we haven't had another one of those disappointing reactions since I began treating this with more importance.

One of my top love languages is Words of Affirmation. I feel most loved when people tell me how they feel about me. It took a long time to get to a place with my dad where he would be open with me and say that he loved me. When I realized this was what I wanted, I was able to articulate it to him in a non-threatening way. He thought I already knew and so he rarely said it. Now that he knows that I like to hear it again and again, he always says it when I see him or talk with him over the phone.

When I want to hear words of affirmation from my husband, I ask him to tell me something sweet and true. It makes him smile, and the things he says to me make my heart flutter. Sometimes you just need to ask for what you want, to show people the way you want to be loved. And, remember to give them love in the way they most enjoy receiving it as well.

A few years ago, I was thinking about my favorite people and what they have in common. I realized that all of them speak all five of the love languages fluently and interchangeably. You can't help but feel loved by someone who is acknowledging what you mean to them in all five ways. The other thing I noticed is that it's easy to express love with each of them. They are all good receivers. It's important to be a good receiver (grateful, acknowledging, thoughtful, etc.) so that people will feel comfortable expressing their love for you. When you're both giving and receiving, you're in the flow, and everyone feels loved.

I highly recommend reading *The Five Love Languages* book for additional insights. The more we know about the ones we love and how they like to be loved, the better friends, partners, and family members we can be. And wouldn't the world be a better place if more people felt genuinely loved?

Must Love Dogs

As I mentioned earlier, I've always been an animal lover. I've had beloved pets for most of my life and enjoyed many years in the company of cats. I also did some puppysitting and housesitting that involved walking, feeding, cuddling with, and caring for dogs. I always enjoyed it, but I felt it on a deeper level when I met my future dog, Zander, while Derek and I were dating.

Zander is a special dog. He's an Italian Greyhound that's very fast and energetic. He also loves lying around the house on his numerous dog beds, which are complete with heating pads. Because of the way he's designed, he has very little body fat or fur to keep himself warm. Luckily, that's not often a challenge living in Southern California, but we keep him as warm and comfy as we can.

Derek has worked with him since he was a puppy and has trained him to do 50 tricks. He's very well-behaved and has the sweetest personality. One of my favorite things about him is that he's a snuggler—not a dog who just lies at the end of the bed, but one who gets under the covers and snuggles in with your body. I smile when I feel him snuggle up to my legs while I'm sleeping. He's also a great cuddler on the couch.

There's something so soulful about Zander. I've learned a lot through being his mommy. Before Derek started teaching me to train him, I had no idea that you had to have boundaries with dogs. I didn't know how sensitive they are to their environments or how important it is to be a leader in the pack of our family. Many of the lessons have carried over into other parts of my life.

When my husband and I were dating, I would watch in awe as he prepared Zander's meals. Not one to simply dump some kibbles into a dish, Derek would cook something special for Zander and mix it with his dog food. He spent more time and energy preparing the dog's meals than I was spending preparing my own. That was an aha moment for me where I realized that even though I don't like to cook, I need to treat myself better and put more thought into my meals. It inspired me to up-level my meal-prep and to be more mindful about eating and the love that can be put into the preparation of food.

Before I met the guy who would become my husband, I was pet-free for several years and chose to remain that way so I would have the freedom and flexibility to travel as far and as long as I wanted. As much as I loved animals, I didn't want to even be responsible for a goldfish for a while. Prior to that time period, I had two kitties, Poohbear and Samantha, that I loved very much for over 15 years. Poohbear was special needs and was on medication and a prescription diet for the last 9–10 years of his life.

Samantha was a feral rescue cat who didn't really feel comfortable around anyone but me. This made traveling difficult as I'd have to find someone to not only feed the kitties and clean their litter boxes, but also to dice up medicine properly, mix it into Poohbear's food, and make sure he ate all of it, while also tolerating Samantha's bad attitude. When they eventually passed away, I decided to wait until it felt right to get my next pet.

Zander won me over immediately with his big eyes, sweet personality, and high energy. He makes me smile every day and is the perfect addition to our family. Instead of feeling like a burden, it's a joy to take care of him and to consider his needs when making our plans. I wish we could take him everywhere we go. When we travel with him, he chooses to build a nest on my lap and will curl up there for hours. He has a few clothes, and we even have birthday parties for him. Suddenly I've become that girl, and I love it! From the looks of it, he does too.

Empowerment and Evolution

Where we're going is more important than where we've been. Let's empower ourselves and our loved ones with the mindset and skillset to rise above any obstacle in order to evolve into the people we're meant to be.

Evolving Beyond Mediocrity

When I was in high school, I thought that the ultimate success in life was to have a predictable job that paid well enough to have a house and live "comfortably." I feel very differently about it now. It's not that I don't want to be comfortable. I do. It's just not the end goal or the way I measure my success at this point in my life. My goal is no longer comfort. It's contribution and impact while feeling happy, fulfilled, and excited about my days.

Sometimes profound realizations come from unexpected places. I remember a conversation where a friend and I were reflecting on what our lives would be like now if we were able to do it over again, taking everything we've learned in life and applying it along the way.

It was a fascinating conversation that led me to the realization that we can collect those learnings and apply them in this powerful moment. We don't need to go back in time. We CAN change the future for the better— with the thoughts we think, the decisions we make, and the actions we take RIGHT NOW.

It's so easy to cling to comfort in order to stay "safe" and to numb ourselves with time-wasters like TV, drugs, alcohol, gossip, negativity, and so on instead of taking the time to really examine our life lessons, vulnerably open ourselves up to our own growth, and use it as a catalyst to transform our lives and the lives of others. The result? Inadvertent mediocrity.

Settling is not for me OR for you. Consciously choosing to do the courageous work to create true positive change is the greatest gift we can give ourselves and our world. I DARE YOU to choose growth. Cheers to our continual evolution!

Every Rose Has its Stem

Roses have a special place in my heart. Yesterday while at the grocery store, I picked out a dozen pink roses to brighten our living room. I feel a surge of positive energy just knowing they're in my home. While stretching on the floor after my at-home workout this morning, I took a look at the roses from a different angle. I realized that their stems are also colorful, vibrant, and strong, not just the blooms themselves. There's beauty in even the bottoms of the petals. I'd never considered appreciating the underside of roses before, but without their powerful, life-giving stems, there would be no buds and no blossoming roses.

It made me think about the current coronavirus pandemic situation and how it's so easy to look for the "roses" and to be disappointed when they aren't immediately obvious. But the truth is that we are all growing stronger and more powerful during these times, and when we bloom as a society, it will be magnificent and worth the wait.

As an entrepreneur navigating the evolving landscape, I'm focusing on the fundamentals and building up my "stems." It may not look impressive to an outsider looking in, but I'm following my inspiration and taking action every day to improve myself and my business. If we take care of our "stems," the roses will appear organically on their own when the time is right and will be powerfully supported by our strength. That, to me, is true power and beauty.

We Girls Can Do Anything. Right, Barbie?

My favorite childhood toy was a Barbie doll. Growing up in the '80s during the heyday for the toy commercials, I loved the jingle, "We girls can do anything. Right, Barbie?" and I fully believed that girls really could do anything because of it. My sister and I loved playing with our Barbie dolls. I remember when I received a Perfume Pretty Whitney for my birthday one year. It was the first brunette Barbie doll I had ever seen, and I thought she was the prettiest one. I felt very connected to that doll because she had brown hair like me. All my life until that moment, I mistakenly thought that I wasn't as pretty or as good as blonde-haired girls. But when I finally saw that Barbie came in brunette, too, it changed things for me. I already loved playing with Barbies, but now I saw myself in that doll and playtime became a lot more interesting.

I know that some people have negativity associated with the look of Barbie dolls. Even though I understand their concerns, for me Barbie represented a world of possibilities that was beyond my immediate environment. Growing up in a small rural town led me to believe that there weren't many options for me as a girl. But Barbie introduced me to the idea that women could be astronauts, veterinarians, dancers, doctors, lead singers, and so much more beyond my imagination at that early age. I loved the idea that you could be both hardworking and glamourous, which was exactly the way I saw my mom. My mom was well respected in her role as a secretary at her office, and she dressed in a professional, yet feminine way.

My Barbies were always starting businesses. I would pretend that my brunette Barbie was starting a gift shop, a newsstand, an advertising company. I had so much fun playing "business" that I would rarely involve my Ken doll. In contrast, my sister and her friends loved to have Barbie going out on dates and hanging around with Ken. Mine got her work done and then went out for a glamourous night on the town.

Looking back, I guess entrepreneurship was always in my blood. Even as a kid, I was constantly coming up with my own little businesses. I had a wreath-making company, a bracelet-braiding company, a Barbie-clothes-making company (they were great unless you wanted to take the custom-made outfits off of your doll), a greeting card company, and more. I had so many ideas, and I was pretty fearless in trying to pull them off. I even went door-to-door trying to sell my handmade greeting cards with limited success.

I often tried to involve others in my ideas. Once after falling off of my bike while second-guessing what another kid was going to do on his (he was out of control and I thought he was going to crash into me), I created hand signals to use while riding bikes, wrote a book about it where I drew out the motion of each signal, and then tried to get the neighborhood kids to adopt the strategy. I was very happy when they played along for an hour or so.

Once I even choreographed a musical in my backyard using my swing set, my audio cassette player, and the demo cassette tape that came free with the purchase of my parents' Ford Tempo. My sister, our friend, and I spent days coming up with the moves for each song and memorizing everything. My plan was to charge the neighborhood kids and parents a quarter in order to come to our backyard and watch the show. This idea horrified my parents who were hardworking and very private people. Disappointed but undeterred, I just came up with different ways to have fun making things while making money, and I guess I never stopped because that's exactly what I'm doing now.

How Does It Feel?

My husband and I have the privilege to speak to thousands of elementary school students each year spreading the love of reading, writing, and creative expression. We love empowering them to explore their interests, create something new, and share it with others to build their reading abilities, confidence, and entrepreneurial skills. During these presentations, we share how we became authors after dreaming about it since we were kids.

One of my favorite questions we get during the Q&A is, "How does it feel to be an author?" The first time this question was posed, I had to think about it for a minute to articulate the overwhelming positive sensations I feel in a way that even the youngest kids could understand. My response was, "It feels like every day is your birthday and you get to be the one giving the presents to everyone." Becoming an author has been a lifelong dream that I let lay dormant inside me for years before I allowed the first book to bloom. Even though it can be challenging being an entrepreneur, it's also the most rewarding thing I've ever done. I feel deep gratitude for the opportunity to creatively express myself in many different forms and to share my inspiration and empowerment with others, especially kids.

When I'm working on a new book, new project, or new dream, I find it very helpful to get in touch with the way I'll feel when the goal is accomplished. I mostly do this through meditation and journaling. It only takes a few minutes every day to visualize and pretend your dream has come true. Once I'm in touch with the way it feels, I can begin my work from a perspective of gratitude that it's already done. This empowers me to be bold and make more progress than I would otherwise.

Let's create a Feeling List that maps out the ways you want to feel about everything in your life. When you really think about it, we desire the things we do because we believe that achieving or receiving them will make us feel happy. Getting clear about how you will feel when your goal is achieved will enable you to create those powerfully positive feelings now and will make it easier for you to ultimately live your dream.

Passion in Action

1. Passion Test – What are your top values?
2. Love List – What are the things you love about yourself?
3. Self-care List – What activities could you do to nurture yourself and help you feel your best?
4. Gratitude List – What are you grateful for?
5. Joy List – What activities do you love? Schedule at least one each week.
6. Feeling List – How do you want to feel about yourself, your relationship, your career, your home, your family, and your legacy?

Passion on Social Media

My favorite social media platform for stoking passion in my everyday life is Facebook. I find it to be the most personal and heartfelt out of all of the big platforms. It's fun to share photos of family and friends, to talk about upcoming events, and to encourage others through comments on their personal achievements. I like that you can add photos, videos, and text to really tell a story about what's going on and how you're feeling. Facebook is the platform from which I receive the most inspiration.

Let's Connect on Facebook

https://www.Facebook.com/SheriFinkFan   @SheriFinkFan

https://www.Facebook.com/WhimsicalWorldBooks   @WhimsicalWorldBooks

PEACE

**Decide what kind of life you really want...
and then, say no to everything that isn't that.**

Peace is a sense of inner calm and centeredness. I've spent a lot of my time working to cultivate the feeling of peace in my life. It's a sense that everything is going to be okay no matter what, a feeling that all is well with the world (even if everything isn't perfect), and a sensation that you can generate your own stillness, which rejuvenates you.

When you have a compelling vision and you're a very driven person, it can be difficult to slow yourself down and enjoy the journey. All the achievements won't matter if you can't be alone with yourself and your thoughts, if your home is a complete disaster area, and if you don't authentically like yourself. No matter how quickly I'm going for a goal, I find that I always get there faster and with a greater sense of fulfillment when I slow down and practice peacefulness in my inner and outer worlds.

Boundaries and Balance

In order for us to feel like we have the time, energy, money, and space to create the lives we really want to live, we need to create and enforce healthy boundaries that enable us to experience a sense of balance. From this open space, we can truly bloom.

Creating Space for More Magic: The Art of Saying "No"

One of the things that I'm working on a lot these days is the art of saying "no." It's astounding to me how many accomplished, amazing people simply don't have the proper tools to say "no" guilt-free with grace and ease. I was one of those people. For too many years, I went along with what other people wanted in hopes of avoiding conflict and keeping them happy. Unfortunately, all it did was keep me unhappy doing things I didn't really want to do instead of doing things that felt meaningful.

There comes a time in our lives when we have to decide what really matters to us. A decision must be made about who we are, what we stand for, and where we're going. To not decide consciously is to decide by default. If we don't set standards for our life and what we'll tolerate, we'll find ourselves deep in drama that seemingly snuck up on us. Sometimes you have to go on a drama diet to realize how peaceful and enjoyable life can really be.

It seems that we're all just running around trying to please other people, often at the expense of ourselves and our dreams. We really don't need permission to say "no" and to protect our schedule from tasks and obligations that shouldn't be ours. Our time and energy are the most precious things we have. Why wouldn't we choose to strategically invest them in tasks and ambitions that are fun, meaningful, and fulfilling to us and our future?

When we don't have a compelling enough vision for our lives, we can get swept up doing things that don't serve us. Sometimes we can get so far off track that we don't even recognize ourselves and our daily routine anymore. It's as if we get on a train when it's standing still and then it picks up speed to the point that it's flying down the track at a velocity that's much too fast for us to safely jump off.

I've noticed in my own life that my bank account grows and my waistline shrinks directly in proportion to my willingness and consistency in saying "no." If I indulge daily in sweet, unhealthy treats and buying things that I don't need just to make me feel good in the moment, those yeses add up and can have negative consequences for my future. That doesn't feel good at all in the long-term.

There's another way. We can be more conscious about how we invest our time and our energy. When an opportunity or invitation is presented to us, we can take a moment to think about how it would feel to actually go through with it while considering our current goals. If the activity is in alignment with those goals, then it feels good and we want to do it. If it will contradict those goals, we'll feel the heaviness of the choice. It feels more like a burden or a chore.

"No" is not a bad word, but many of us treat it like it is by rarely ever saying it. When we do say it, we usually add an apology. There's no need to apologize for choosing to pursue your dreams or invest time in yourself, no matter how entitled others feel to your time.

A tool that I learned and like to use in response to opportunities that don't excite me is, "I'd love to, but it's just not possible." If I already have plans, I say something like, "I'd love to, but I have a prior commitment that evening." Either way, I'm acknowledging the request and letting them know that I won't be participating. The communication is clear, respectful, and direct. There's no room to wiggle a "yes" out of me because I've clearly communicated that it's a "no."

Boundaries: Reclaiming Your Time, Energy, and Space

One of the most valuable things that I've learned (and continue to learn) is how and when to set boundaries in my life and business. Setting boundaries is a healthy way to respect yourself and others, but most of us avoid it because we don't know how. We haven't considered what our standards are for our lives and, therefore, don't know exactly when a boundary is crossed. In some cases, we know we need to set a boundary, but don't do it because we feel awkward.

It's true that it can feel uncomfortable to talk with someone about inappropriate behavior, but it'll feel much more uncomfortable to allow it to continue and diminish your self-worth in the process.

There have been many times in my life when I didn't want to risk feeling awkward, being mistaken in my interpretations, or making someone else feel bad. And every time that I didn't speak up, I felt scared, sad, resentful, or seething inside. I was disappointed in myself. Instead of using it as an opportunity to build a bridge, I felt the need to protect myself by building a wall.

I've regretted not addressing things as soon as they happen because they not only continued, they got worse. Inspirational thought leader Robin Sharma teaches that "you can say anything to anyone so long as you say it with respect." I believe he's right.

Examples of opportunities to set boundaries:

1.   **When someone wants a favor from you and you want to help them, but they haven't done the necessary work on their part to make it easy for you.** People often ask me for help promoting something to my friends and Fans through social media. And I used to spend lots of time trying to figure out the value of what they were offering, the emotional connection of why it mattered, the call to action, and the link that gets them where they want them to go.

As I became more blessed in my business and found myself busier as I aspired to do more meaningful work, I realized that I couldn't continue investing my time in things that other people could be doing for themselves. So, now I ask them to write the post with the link and send it to me so I can copy, paste, tweak, and share it. I teach them how to craft more meaningful posts and save my time to invest in other projects. It's a win-win.

2.   **When someone wants to borrow something from you that you feel uncomfortable lending.** It could be money, your car, a book, a pair of shoes, whatever it is, if it doesn't feel good to allow them to borrow it, say "no." I learned this lesson the hard way in college when I went against my better judgment and loaned my car to a friend who drove to a club, got into a fight, acquired a huge shoeprint on the side of my car, and had it taken away and locked in an impound lot. The "friend" never repaid me for the damage done to my car, not to mention the horrible experience of having to call my dad and beg for his help to get my car back.

I vowed never to go against my instincts on this topic again. Save yourself the money and the headache by declining this boundary-crossing request from the beginning. And, if your friend doesn't like that you said "no," that's okay. Maybe they're not looking out for your best interests after all.

3. **When someone sits or stands too close to you or touches you in an overly familiar way that makes you feel uncomfortable.** If I have a bad feeling while I'm in an elevator with someone, I will get out on the next floor and wait for another one with a less creepy vibe. No one has the right to touch you for any reason. You don't have to go along with anything to make someone else feel comfortable. Let them get embarrassed. If they're crossing a boundary, it's your right to tell them to stop. Speak up early and often so they will leave you alone.

4. **When someone wants to take the credit for the work you've done.** Almost everyone has had the experience of working really hard on a project only to discover later that someone else claimed it was their idea, their effort, or their results. It's perfectly acceptable to speak up and acknowledge your contributions. Own your ideas, your efforts, and your work. It can be done with grace and respect, and without tearing down the credit-stealer. I regret the times that I didn't speak up when it happened to me in my career. It's as if I was telling myself that it wasn't okay to tell the truth and stand up for myself. I don't make myself wonder if I'll do the right thing anymore, I just do it. Once the credit-stealer realizes that you won't silently sulk about it, they'll find someone else's spotlight to steal.

5. **When someone wants you to work for free.** There are limited occasions when it's acceptable to gift your product or service to others. It's not okay for others to expect you to sacrifice your time, energy, income, products, or services for them to constantly receive freebies. It's one thing to choose to be generous and donate your time, products, or services. It's a completely different thing to feel guilted or manipulated into doing so. If it doesn't feel right, don't do it. If you did something out of guilt in the past, forgive yourself and set a boundary moving forward. Respecting the value of your time and energy will greatly build your self-confidence and self-esteem, as well as help free up your time to focus on income-generating activities.

Today I was listening to best-selling business author Brendon Burchard while I was working out at the gym, and he said something that really spoke to me. He said, "emotions and excellence are contagious," and I believe that to be true. I also think that expectations can be contagious. As we spend time with people who hold us to a higher standard, we tend to do the same for ourselves. After being surrounded by those feelings for a while, it becomes a habit to think a certain way. Done consistently enough, those thoughts and actions shape our personality, and the decisions made from that space shape our lives and our contributions to society.

Make Time for Your Dreams

It can be difficult to get started on your dreams, especially if you feel like you've been derailed or struggled in the past. Even writing this book has been challenging for me because I have long periods where my schedule is so full that I don't have time to focus on it. It's an important goal that aligns with my values, my life vision, and my purpose. But it's so easy to prioritize all of the more urgent projects and to have weeks go by without making any substantive progress on my book.

What I'm finding is that I need to allocate time in my calendar to write. It's not going to happen every day, but even a few hours a week will get me where I want to go and will eventually lead to you (the reader) holding this book in your hands.

It's easy to put yourself and your self-care on the backburner when you're busy taking care of everything and everyone else. I know in my heart how important it is to meditate and work out, but I've still allowed other activities to become my priority for the past six months. I feel the impact of those micro-decisions to skip my meditation and shorten my workouts now. The choices I made aren't 100% in alignment with my values and my vision for my life.

I want to be a woman who makes conscious decisions with the long-term impact in mind. It is important for me to be a woman who is fit, healthy, confident, energetic, and who is calm, clear, and compassionate with herself and others. Prioritizing my self-care helps me be that woman. So, I need to take another look at what I'm making more important than my health and well-being and change it. I think most of us are happier when we feel healthy. That level of aliveness and vibrancy is crucial to living a productive and fulfilling life.

There's no shortcut to greatness. It takes planning, discipline, and hard work. I think that's what makes it so worthwhile. I just received the proof of my newest book, *World of Whimsy with the Little Unicorn,* my eleventh book and my first board book for babies. As I held it in my hands for the first time yesterday, I started to feel emotional and felt myself tearing up. It's amazing to me that I've written 11 books (in addition to this one). As a kid, I dreamt of being a writer, and every now and then I realize that I'm living that dream. My books have all been written over the past nine years, through some of the saddest and happiest times in my life so far. I've had many moments that were hard, when I felt like giving up. But I held tight to my dream and, on days like today, I'm incredibly grateful that I persisted through the challenges.

My goal in life was never to be mediocre. I've always wanted to make a massive positive difference in the world, even when the enormity of that vision scared me. I want to do things that I've never seen done before and to reach people in new ways. And I want to have lots of fun along the way. Sometimes well-meaning people have discouraged me from dreaming "too big" and being "unrealistic." It used to make me mad, but now I understand that they were trying to protect me from disappointment because they didn't believe those things were possible for themselves. If they couldn't do it, they definitely didn't think that I could. I've learned not to take it personally and not to let other people's limitations limit me.

I have a plan for my life and I keep taking action in that direction every day. My passion for making a difference, creating things I love, and living a juicy, fulfilling life is much stronger than any bouts of doubt or fear I experience. I have an important mission on this planet, and it calls to me when I feel lost or unmotivated.

It can also be difficult to see yourself clearly. People may look at you and your success and marvel. Meanwhile, you might only be focusing on the gap between where you are and where you want to go. It's valuable to invest time each month to reflect on your accomplishments and to acknowledge your victories.

I created a daily journal to help me with this called *My Bliss Book: An Inspirational Journal for Daily Dream Building and Extraordinary Living*, and I find that it gives me a more balanced perception of myself as I strive to achieve my big goals. There are no insignificant accomplishments. Some days just going to the gym, showering, and doing the laundry are victories. Other days, you may achieve much more. Owning your victories will increase your confidence and empower you to keep going when you're less motivated.

Is It a "Hell Yes?"

As I mentioned earlier, I've learned a lot over the years from Jack Canfield. One of the most valuable lessons I've learned is to determine what is a "Hell Yes" in my life and treat everything else as a "Hell No."

In our society, we are bombarded by requests for our time, energy, and money, which directly impacts our sanity. If we say "yes" to everyone and everything, we'll absolutely burn ourselves out and have nothing left to take care of our basic necessities. So, Jack teaches that when presented with an opportunity, potential purchase, to-do, etc., to ask ourselves if this is a "Hell Yes" for us. You can tell it is when the idea excites you and you can see how it fits in with the rest of your plans and goals. Even if it's a boring task that brings you closer to your dream coming true, that's a "Hell Yes."

In contrast, a "Hell No" is anything else. So, if it doesn't knock your socks off to think about doing or buying or going wherever it is, then that's a "Hell No" for you. That doesn't mean that you actually say, "Hell No." You politely decline and refuse to allow yourself to feel guilty for not participating. A lot of parents want to be active participants at their children's schools. But if you have four children, two jobs, and a myriad of other responsibilities, there just might not be time to head up the school's bake sale. This is an opportunity for you to either say "yes" out of joy of getting to do it or to say "no" out of respect for yourself and your time. It's an easy way to make decisions on what to commit to and what to pass on.

In my own life, there were many times where I felt like I "had to" say "yes" for fear of hurting someone's feelings or to avoid the awkwardness associated with saying "no." I no longer feel that way. I recognize that our time, money, and energy are precious and finite. If I run around town doing everything everyone else wants, my own life will be in shambles and I will resent everyone I said "yes" to. But it wasn't their fault for asking, it was mine for saying "yes" when I should have said "no."

Sometimes when that's happened, it's because I didn't feel like I had the tools or the right words to say "no" while maintaining the dignity of the asker. I cared more about the way they felt than the way I felt about doing something I didn't want to. (Can I get an amen?) When declining, always be truthful (don't say you are going somewhere else when you intend to stay home), don't apologize (you're not doing anything wrong by declining an invitation), and don't make excuses (it's really nobody's business why the answer is "no"—"no" is a full sentence). Be kind and firm if they try to ask you again.

Don't be tempted to get out of the conversation by telling someone you'll think about it when you know deep down that the answer is going to be "no" regardless of how long you consider it. You're not doing them any favors by stringing them along. If you say "no" upfront, you release yourself from the burden of following up and delivering the "no" later (ugh) and you enable them to start looking for someone else instead of pinning all of their hopes on you.

There's never a need to get into an in-depth conversation or analysis of your motivations. You have your own life to lead, and you know what's best for you. Keep your commitment to yourself to only sign up for and buy things that are truly a "Hell Yes" and your energy level will soar. You can use all that juicy energy to work on your dreams.

Here are a few ways to politely decline and extricate yourself from sticky situations that aren't a "Hell Yes" for you:

"I'd love to, but it's just not possible."

"Thanks for the invitation, but I have another commitment for that day/night."

"I won't be able to attend. Thanks for thinking of me."

"No, thank you. Wishing you all the best."

"That doesn't work for me. Thanks anyway."

In addition to your newfound free time and increased energy level, you'll also discover that being kind, direct, and firm with your "no" leads to people respecting you more. You'll receive fewer mediocre requests when people realize that it has to be truly important in order to get you onboard. It's a wonderful, peaceful, calm, and confident state to live in when you know that you can decline any request with dignity and grace and not take on other people's dramas or emergencies. Is there something or someone in your life who you need to say "no" to? What will you do with the time you free up by saying "no" to things that don't sing to your soul?

Energy and Environment

The environments in which we spend the most time have the greatest impact on our energy. We can choose to simplify and enhance our environments to increase our energy, to provide a sense of peace and well-being, and to support us in our goal to live our dreams.

Your Home Is Your Sanctuary

Years ago, I had a subconscious desire to fill up my life, my home, my mailbox, and my mind with lots of things. I think it originated from growing up modestly and subsequently placing value on having a lot of stuff. I didn't realize at that time that everything we allow into our lives has an energetic cost associated with it, and often a physical cost, too. Surrounding ourselves with stuff and to-dos can also be a subconscious way to hide amid the clutter. There's always a distraction that keeps us from going inward, feeling our feelings, and truly knowing ourselves. It also prevents us from starting the most intimidating projects that will help achieve our dreams.

When we realize that we don't need so many things and that our belongings and obligations don't define us, it can be both exciting and terrifying to be liberated. Going through our junk forces us to process the past and to make different decisions about the future. Sometimes that includes admitting that we've filled our bodies, homes, and schedules up with things that didn't matter for so long that we can hardly recognize who we've become.

On the other side, there's an adrenaline rush that comes from freeing ourselves of these burdens. The less we have in our environments, the less we have to take care of, clean, mend, and manage. I remember reading Peter Walsh's book, *It's All Too Much,* and embracing his philosophy on decluttering. I find that it applies beyond just our homes. When we only keep the things that matter, it simplifies our lives. With space comes clarity. And, my home, my office, and my life are much more peaceful when I manage the things in them well.

A strategy that works well for me is to handle things and make decisions about them the day they enter my home. Just investing five or fewer minutes on this each day keeps the dreaded piles away and makes me feel good about decisively handling my mail. I used to let it pile up and defer the decision-making to the point that just looking at the pile of paper would give me anxiety.

When the mail arrives, I sort it the same day, recycle everything I don't need, contact the companies sending junk mail and request to be removed from their lists, and take action on any mail I need. I may hold onto Fan letters for a few days and then schedule a chunk of time to respond to them all at once. Things I need to keep for reference get filed immediately.

I'm very mindful of the things in my space that I see every day and the energy I feel from them. I want to be surrounded by happy memories of being with my family, fun adventures, and fulfilling accomplishments. My home is my sanctuary, and I want it to nurture and nourish me to be my best self and create my best work. Anything that doesn't bring out my best isn't worth having visible in my home and, most times, isn't worth having at all.

For a long time, I even kept clothes that I hated. These were things that looked good in the store, but weren't quite right for me when I tried them on at home. They had their own section in the back of my closet where they seemed to multiply. Every day I would see them in my closet and feel bad about myself for wasting money. I came to realize that the real waste was continuing to give these superfluous items space in my life. Once I donated them, I felt great giving new items to people who could use them, plus I freed up valuable closet real estate available for clothes I really loved.

Since doing that massive clean out, I'm more selective about the things I buy and add to my home. I only want to own things that I love, so I don't buy a lot anymore. The things I do invest in, I really appreciate and take care of. I've followed this process for just about everything in my life now. It feels so different and refreshing to live in a home filled only with things I love, are useful, and elevate my spirit.

I handle my email inbox in much the same way. I used to subscribe to everything hoping to learn new things. Over time, I realized that spending so much time reading emails was distracting me from time I could invest in learning something that was actually valuable. I no longer feel like I'm going to miss something. If I'm meant to know it, it'll find me another way.

I unsubscribe from every email that doesn't consistently help me, bring me joy, or add value to my life. It's wonderful to open my email and only find messages that matter. I still sometimes receive spam and I simply report it to my email provider and block the sender. Nothing more to worry about.

Living simply and minimizing distractions in my home gives me the space to let my creativity run wild. I feel more energetic, innovative, and determined. I have more time to create and dream because I'm spending less time cleaning and organizing.

Everyone is unique, and I feel your home should be custom-tailored to suit your needs. For example, my husband and I both love to dress up in costumes for our business, for our creative endeavors (plays, shows, etc.), and for cosplay fun. We're the only people I know who have an entire closet dedicated to costumes. I love that about us. Our costume closet is a magical place where I can become anyone I want. Maybe you like to paint and can dedicate a space in your home as a studio. The whole idea is to let go of the belongings that don't serve the person you're becoming and to use that space for things and activities that bring you joy, whatever that may be for you.

Similarly, when my schedule is too full, I don't have time for writing. Writing is an activity that requires effort and is incredibly fulfilling for me. If I don't make time for it, I feel off-balance and creatively in a slump. Because I know that writing is important for my well-being, I schedule blocks of time to do it on my calendar.

Working out is the same way for me, extremely important and easy to skip if I don't plan my workouts in advance and put them on my calendar. My life just goes better when I work out and write at least several times each week.

Minimalism Life Makeover

Why is it sometimes hard to let go of things even if you haven't used them in years (or ever) and you know you probably won't use them in the future, nor miss them when they're gone? When you're busy living your life, raising a family, growing a business, and so on, things can accumulate and multiply. Physical, mental, and emotional clutter sometimes pile up in all of our lives.

It sometimes feels easier in the short-term to let the stuff stay, and we become comfortable in our clutter-filled environment. It can be difficult to make decisions that would enable us to let things go, justifying our resistance with questions like, "What if I need this someday?" In most cases, we won't, and the quality of our lives could be dramatically improved by letting go of superfluous items, thoughts, people, and obligations that no longer fit the life we want to live or the person we're becoming.

I remember when I was moving years ago, and I walked around my place realizing that I didn't really want to take any of the furniture I had with me to start my "new" life in a different state. Most of the items were purchased from yard sales or gifted as hand-me-downs from friends and family while I was in college. Those items were perfect for me when I got them, but they didn't fit the direction I was growing anymore. And I definitely didn't want to pay to move them across the country with me!

So I decided to only take the items I loved or actually used. It was a little scary at first to let go of so many things at once. It was also liberating and exciting to start fresh by consciously choosing the items for my environment. When I moved into my new place 3,000 miles away, I didn't miss anything I donated or threw away. Instead, I had a beautiful, light-filled, clutter-free space to enjoy.

I find myself needing to do an annual spruce-up where I question the utility of things in my life, business, and environment. If it doesn't bring me joy or serve an active purpose, I let go of it and create space for more magic and things that make me smile in my life. I always feel so refreshed and energized when I'm done.

Even with this awareness and commitment, evolution is a process. Sometimes it's other people's things that they haven't let go of that clutter our lives. When I first moved in with my husband, the garage and most of the closets in the house were full of old things that belonged to his mother. She had been storing them there for years. Throughout our first year together, the garage leaked and flooded a few times during heavy rains, soaking through the cardboard boxes and making their contents mostly unusable. And yet, there they were taking up valuable space in our garage.

One day I looked out the window and saw my beautiful SUV sitting in the driveway and thought about the value of my vehicle and how it was exposed to the elements, vulnerable to drivers on the street, and how much I dreaded moving it early in the morning on street sweep day. I was using a lot of energy worrying about my car being there when it really belonged in our garage.

Once I realized that we were (by inaction) making someone else's old belongings more important than protecting one of our most expensive assets (the SUV that I owned outright), I talked with Derek about it and he agreed that it was a fixable situation.

We scheduled a day to clean up her storage spaces in order to create space for her to keep some of the stuff she was storing in our garage. It turned out that many of the things there could be thrown away and organized to make room for more. We even bought her a hanging rack for all of her clothes she wanted to salvage.

Then, we dedicated a day to helping her sort through all of the boxes in the garage. It was an arduous process where we'd lift one box and two others would fall. None of the boxes were labeled so their contents were always a surprise.

Box by box, we helped her decide to throw away two large dumpsters worth of items that were no longer useful to anyone. She donated a few bags of things and kept the rest, which we moved into the storage space we had tidied up for her. We even moved a heavy-duty shelving unit that wouldn't fit into our vehicles by pushing it on a small cart over two blocks to her storage space. We carried and placed everything in the storage room and then we finally went home for much-needed showers. Covered in dirt, dust, and dried sweat, we looked and felt like we had run a Tough Mudder!

Determined to create space for me, our future family, and our business needs, we also helped her clean out all of the closets. Now our closets are no longer cluttered with things from the past. We have full usage of our space for our future, and that feels amazing.

We had the garage power washed and painted the next day. It looked like a totally different garage! And, the best part is that both of our SUVs can be parked safely in our garage together, which was a huge relief for me. I didn't realize how much energy it was draining from me worrying about the safety and security of my car in the driveway. Now his mom's items are clean, organized, and stored properly and safely in a way she can actually find what she's looking for—a happy ending for everyone.

1. What areas of your life are you (through action or inaction) prioritizing something that's not really worth the priority?

2. What would you like this aspect of your life to be like?

3. What steps could you take to eliminate the energy drain and make it right?

4. How will you feel once the work has been done and the transition has been made?

It may be difficult to ask for what you want and do the physical work necessary to fulfill your vision, but I promise that it will be worth the effort. I feel grateful every day that I park in my pristine garage. Now it's an energy booster instead of an energy drainer.

Let Go and Grow

Last year, I dedicated a weekend to undertaking a major project, and I accomplished my goal even beyond my expectations. I wanted to take five bins of photos, albums, scrapbooks, and frames from storage and consciously choose the ones to keep and throw away or recycle. I wanted to get rid of the old albums and organize the photos chronologically into new albums and photo boxes. It was a beast of a task physically, mentally, and emotionally. I uncovered photos that surprised me and had a good cry about some things from the past and people who have passed. It was a really good experience for me to get closure and honor my history. I had so many photos that made me feel bad. Why was I keeping those?

By letting go of thousands of photos and aging albums, I was able to sculpt something beautiful and meaningful from the slab of memories I had previously held onto by default. Now I'm happy that the photos I consciously chose to keep are properly stored and easily accessible to me for my enjoyment. I thought I would need three or four huge photo albums and a photo box. Turns out I only needed one large album and one photo box because I did such a good job of paring them down.

One of the items I struggled with was old scrapbooks. I had ten of them. I remember investing a lot of time, energy, and money into making them years ago. They seemed very important back then so I initially thought I would just take them back to storage (they took up one and a half of the five bins). Then I talked with my husband about it, and he gave me the idea to take pictures of the pages and let go of the physical books.

At first, I thought that was too extreme, that I "needed" to keep my art projects. Then I looked through them and felt nothing. They used to bring me joy, or at least what I thought was joy back then. But I realized that they had served their purpose, and I chose to let them go. That day I made peace with the past so I could be fully in the present.

I brought the bins to my joy-filled home and sun-filled office. The energy here is powerful and positive and makes it easier to notice when things don't match it anymore. This would have been harder to notice in the dusty, dark gray storage facility. I was also motivated to finish quickly so I could return my office to the beautiful, peaceful space it usually is.

It's funny when we think about the symbols we choose to keep in order to remember the past, even the things we hold onto that remind us of negative experiences. It felt very satisfying to release literally 50–75 pounds of stored stuff that wasn't useful to me anymore. It was a heavy burden of pain, guilt, shame, and regret from the past, and it felt liberating to release it. I knew that it was the right choice for me.

It helped that I waited until now, when I'm the happiest I've ever been, to take on my storage project. I could make decisions from a place of joy, free from the physical, mental, and emotional burden of the past, and trust in myself to make the right decisions.

Up-Level Your Environments

Our homes and offices are where we spend the majority of our time. Because we see the space every day, we may not pay attention to the way it looks until everything is in piles and there's a big mess to clean up. Our homes are the canvases of our lives. If we have space to create, to play, to love, and to live, we have happier, more fulfilling lives. When we're embarrassed to open the door because of what lurks behind, we can't help but feel smaller in life and ashamed of the mess we've created. That daily energy drain has an impact on us whether we know it or not.

Back when I was a clutterbug, I kept my place neat and clean, but there were mountains of organized clutter everywhere. It wasn't until I saw my living room in the background of a photo that I realized that my collections had grown a bit out of control. Clearing things out can feel overwhelming, but wow, what a difference having open space makes!

When I walk into my home, I want it to feel like my sanctuary. I want my bathroom to feel like a spa and my office to feel like a studio. I do best in spaces that are filled with light and minimal objects. I like the few items that I choose for my spaces to be hand-selected because of the meaning they have for me, the happy memories they invoke, or the joy they bring me (like a photo of my family having the time of our lives on vacation).

Too much of a good thing can become a bad thing. If you collect something, it might be nice to have a few of those items. Depending on the size of the objects, maybe even a hundred of them is fine. But when your collections start to take over your environment, it might be time to take another look and decide what your space is for. If you're happy turning your home into a museum that houses your collection of vintage tiki mugs, keep going full-steam ahead feeling confident that you made that choice consciously. If you'd rather have space for your kids to play, for your spouse to stretch out in the recliner, and for you to easily be able to enter your closet and come out feeling stunning; it might be time to pare down the collection.

After I sold my house, I lived in a basement apartment (under my landlord's house) that was so tiny that it didn't have a bathroom door. There was simply no space for it. But even though it was a small space, I kept it immaculate with very little clutter, which made it easy to clean regularly. It was a beautiful space even though it was semi-below ground. The best part of that place (besides the affordable rent) was the proximity to the ocean, which was less than a block away. I fell asleep listening to the waves and would set timers to run outside and see the sunset each day I was home.

Eventually, I outgrew the space and wanted something more spacious where I could actually entertain friends (and have space for a couch and a bathtub). When the time was right, I found the perfect new apartment with four times the space (further from the beach). My first step toward creating a beautiful, inspiring, and relaxing space was to come up with a color palette. I love beachy furniture and the color teal and decided that would be my look.

My mom visited to help me furnish and decorate my new place. I already had a beautiful bedroom suite and desk that I brought from my previous residence, but I needed a dining room table and chairs, a couch, a comfy chair, and a patio set. We shopped like our lives depended on it, visiting every store that might have something of interest, price comparing online, and ultimately purchasing and assembling furniture for my new place. We also bought curtain rods, hung a shower curtain, and hemmed curtains (my mom's handiwork). By the end of the week, we were exhausted, but I was overjoyed to have such a beautiful space in which to live and work.

Moving to my new apartment and making it my home, with the generous help of my mother, enhanced my environment and gave me a burst of energy. Because I wasn't hanging onto a bunch of old stuff that didn't bring me joy, I could choose items to bring into my space that did. My whole world improved as a result. I felt joy coming home to my relaxing, neat, and cozy sanctuary. Just walking into my living room gave me a sense of peace and freedom.

How would it feel to have a home that only contains things that you love or find useful? What would it be like to relax into a bubble bath at home without seeing all the bottles of shampoo, half-used tubes of toothpaste, and hairballs that congregate in a cluttered bathroom? What would it feel like to walk into your office and feel creative, present, and alive, ready to change the world? How would it feel to be able to confidently open your door to guests at the last minute without running around in a mad panic hiding things in closets, drawers, and closed rooms? How confident would you feel in that kind of space?

What items do you have in your environment that are just there (not bringing you joy or being a help to you)? What items do you have that bring you feelings of unease, sadness, or anger? What would you like to change about your space to bring you more peace and joy? What's one thing you can start with this week that will brighten your place and your day? Is there a color that you love that you'd like to incorporate into your space?

Make a wish list of changes you'd like to make in order to convert your home into your sanctuary, your bathroom into a spa, and your office into a studio. Do one each week until you achieve your vision and your place smiles back at you. Don't worry if there are a lot of things you want to change. It doesn't have to be perfect, just perfectly you. Keep imagining your up-leveled space and keep taking steps toward it. You'll get there and it will be worth it!

Thank You for Being a Friend

When I was in school, I had a lot of acquaintances, but didn't feel like I had any true friends. That's partly because of immature falling outs with friends in earlier grades and partly because I had a boyfriend. It's also because there were things happening in my home that I didn't want anyone to know about.

My parents finally separated when I was in eighth grade. It was definitely for the best. They are both good people, but they were not compatible with each other. It was a difficult time for me, and I didn't really want to share it with kids who went to my school. I didn't have anyone that I trusted on that level, so I found my own pseudo-friends on television every night when I watched *The Golden Girls*.

I loved each of those ladies. They were funny, smart, unique, and loving. Even though they weren't technically related (other than mother-daughter pair Sophia and Dorothy), they were a happy family. It was probably weird for a teenager to fall in love with a sitcom about women over 60, but there I was tuning in every night and falling asleep to the happy sounds of their theme song.

It really helped me through that time in my life. I appreciated the way that watching the show made me feel, like everything would be okay no matter what, and that was a reassurance I desperately needed back then. It's one of the reasons why I only want to create content (books, talks, and music) that uplifts people in hopes that they'll be reassured when they most need it as well.

Silence and Synchronicity

Immersing ourselves in moments of solitude and silence can enhance the peace we feel at home and in the world. By cultivating an inner connection with ourselves, we're better grounded and energized to pursue our goals.

Journaling

When I journal, I listen to myself and I feel better because I'm not seeking attention, validation, or approval from anyone else. It feels like such a luxury to spend this time with myself and fully hear my thoughts and feelings. When I give myself what I need, I feel less grumpy, scared, and needy. It's empowering to take care of myself and the effects are cumulative. If I just do what I need to each day, it all adds up to a well-balanced, happy, abundant, and fulfilled me. That's the best reward of all!

Enjoy the Silence

I did something a little crazy a few months ago. I turned off the notifications on my phone. Not just the audible alerts, but also the visual badges that signal that there's a new interaction or message on an app. I did it on all my apps, email, etc. except for texts and phone calls (which are also silenced but show a visual notification).

I took drastic action because the constant lure of the glowing and chiming distractions had me continually picking up my phone. It was making it really difficult to focus on my writing, or anything of significance, because my attention was constantly divided.

I started by silencing my phone for a day while I was writing. I enjoyed the quiet so much that I left it off for a week. I realized I was still picking up my phone every few minutes (now I'm blushing…maybe you can relate?) and decided to turn the badges off. In my line of work, no one dies if I don't write back immediately or read their message the moment it's posted. So I'm quite enjoying my newfound freedom and quiet.

My writing has benefited with more words per day and more fulfillment. I feel a lot more productive. I'm not as compelled to touch my phone as often (it was tough at first, though!). I feel significantly more creative because I'm not multi-tasking and distracting myself from what matters. I still love my social media, I just engage with it in intentional doses rather than instantly by default. I already feel more relaxed, and I'm accomplishing more in a day. I feel better in general when I'm intentional with my time and energy. Before, it was easy to start scrolling and have thirty minutes disappear. Now, when I allow myself the time to engage with social media after my most important tasks are done, I achieve my goals, use my time wisely, and make my social media minutes count.

Synchronicity: Hold on Tight to Your Dreams

I've experienced too many miracles to believe that life is a series of random events and experiences. It's easy to jump to that conclusion during times that I feel out of alignment with myself and my ambitions. I've gone through long periods of time where I felt like everything I was trying to do was an uphill battle, like it was a struggle just to get through the day. I still witnessed opportunities unfolding around me, but they weren't the ones that I felt that I really wanted or that would take me in the direction that I mistakenly thought I wanted to go. That's where hindsight can be so helpful. Looking back, I can see that the reason I didn't excel in some of those endeavors despite all of my efforts was that I wasn't meant to climb those particular mountains.

The universe conspired to keep me on the ground rather than start the climb at that time because those mountains weren't the ones for me. And, in my inexperience, I would see a mountain (any mountain) and start climbing without thinking about where the journey would take me. Would that job take me where I wanted to be in 10–20 years? Would continuing to date that guy who doesn't make my heart flutter lead me to a blissful relationship five years from now? Would choosing that apartment give me the peace and creative space I craved and be a place I could call home in three years?

What I was lacking at times was clarity. Without knowing exactly what I wanted, I attracted a grab bag of opportunities, but not all of them were right for me. The goals and visions I had since I was a child were crystal clear for me. I knew from a very early age that I wanted to live in California. It seemed like a world away from where I was growing up. I had never met anyone from California in person, but I did have two friends who got to go to Disneyland with their families when we were young. I would ask them so many questions about everything they did, saw, and experienced on their trips. I watched television shows that were based in Southern California and daydreamed about seeing palm trees in person (they still make me smile).

I would excitedly tell my family that one day I was going to live in California. My five-year-old self's boisterous proclamation and endless enthusiasm for all things Californian was often met with skepticism from my well-meaning, but not big-dreaming, relatives. They would constantly try to talk me out of it saying things like, "California? Ugh. Why would you ever want to live there?" and "Don't you know they have earthquakes?" Sometimes I would question my judgement for a day or so, but then came to the conclusion that California was the place for me.

With my greater grown-up perspective, I can understand that my family members weren't necessarily trying to discourage me from my dream. None of them had ever been beyond the East Coast, and many of them hadn't been beyond the borders of Virginia. All they knew about California was what they had heard on the news, and that isn't the most flattering representation of any state. To them, saying I wanted to live in California was like saying I wanted to live on the moon.

In their experience, it didn't pay to have big dreams like that because they would find a reason not to achieve the goal and then feel crushed that they didn't get it. As hardworking as they were, they couldn't see a world in which it was possible for them to live in a place that was different than the one they already knew. By discounting my dream, they were trying to protect me from the disappointment that they thought I would inevitably face if my dream didn't come true. But they clearly didn't know what I was capable of. Defending my dream to them made me even more determined to make it come true. And in 2003, that's exactly what I did when I finally seized the opportunity to make the big cross-country move.

I had an opportunity to move a year earlier but chose to turn it down in order to finish my master's degree. I researched the universities in the local area and discovered that my credits would not easily transfer into any of their degree programs. Earning my master's degree was one of my big goals, and I would have had to start completely over if I were to move then. It was a hard decision to make, but I let it go and reassured myself that if I was meant to be a California Girl, then another opportunity would present itself when the time was right. Boy, I'm glad I did.

When the second chance arrived, I was ecstatic. I said "yes" immediately and then realized how much work needed to be done before the big move in just 30 days. I had to give my notice at my current job, give away a lot of things that I didn't want to take, pack everything else, learn how to transport a vehicle and two kitties across the country, turn in my other leased car to the dealership, find a great place to live in California even though I was currently in Virginia, say goodbye to all of my friends, and the hardest one of all, tell my family.

You would think that after almost 20 years of saying that I was going to live in California, that it would be easy to say it one more time and really mean it, but it was difficult. I wasn't as close to my immediate family then as I am now, but I spent a lot of time with them and I knew they wouldn't be as happy as I was about my decision. There were a lot of tears, and we all had an ugly cry. After that, even though they were nervous for me, they were onboard and supported my dream. Telling my family made it real for me. Even though for years I would check the weather online for Southern California and imagine enjoying 70-degree days instead of 38-degree snow days, doing all of the preparation with a real deadline was a lot of work.

The synchronicities were all around. I had wanted this to happen all my life and that desire was so strong that I could almost see it, feel it, and taste it. For the next 30 days, I had incredible energy for getting the tasks done. Although it wasn't easy, it was as if everything aligned for me to make this huge undertaking simpler than it could've been. I was on cloud nine and almost crying every day because I was so happy that I was finally going to live my dream. Nothing could stop me because I was in my joy. Whatever I needed to do, I was committed to figuring it out. Plus, petty annoyances that seemed to drive me crazy in the past just didn't matter as I strove to make every moment with my loved ones special and to plot the best course for this next chapter in my life.

It's not easy to upend your life and change everything. But in my case, it was worth it. I found moving to California to be an incredible experience. There were so many things that I took for granted living in Northern Virginia—I didn't see the beauty all around me anymore. I was working so hard on my degree and my multiple jobs that I didn't take as good care of myself or take any time to enjoy the roses.

When I arrived in California, everything was fresh and new. Suddenly, I had full presence and noticed everything around me. I was in awe that many flowers bloom here in the winter, that I never had to shovel snow out from around my car, and that I lived so close to Disneyland. I saw infinite possibilities because I had to pay attention again. I was no longer in a rut. I had to be fully present just to figure out how to get to the grocery store. Everything in my life felt alive and energetic.

I started becoming a better receiver for the synchronicities that were flowing into my life. Because I had achieved this monumental goal, I valued myself more. I began working out at the gym in my apartment complex and chose to only buy new things that I absolutely loved. After a few months of working out, I purged 90% of my closet as I realized that those clothes didn't physically or emotionally fit the new me. I no longer wanted to hide in dark suits and pantyhose, I wanted to stand out in vibrant colors and open-toed shoes. I had fun shopping for the first time in years, looking for things that fit the new me and my new life in California.

As I became more confident and felt safer, I actually started to like being in photos. I wanted to try new foods and new adventures—do things that I was too scared or self-conscious to do in the past. Moving to California helped me see myself and everything around me in a new light, changing my life for the better, just like I dreamed it would when I was a little girl.

If you have a big dream (and I hope you have multiple), spend a little time each day feeling what it will be like when your dream has come true. Think about how you'll feel waking up knowing that your dream is real. Visualize looking through your own eyes and see it from your perspective as if you're living the dream right now. What does it taste like? What does it smell like? What does it sound like? What does it feel like? Give yourself a dose of that pick-me-up every day and before you know it, you'll begin attracting opportunities that will ultimately lead you to the achievement of that goal or something even juicier.

Freedom and Forgiveness

Forgiving ourselves and others can be a very challenging and rewarding endeavor. When we forgive, we release the attachment to the feelings and thoughts about what happened so that we are free to fully move forward into the future.

Dealing with Disappointment

I really hate to be disappointed. I often see the best in people and situations and move forward in good faith. Not wanting to face your reality doesn't change reality, and avoiding it usually makes it worse. Sometimes I discover (later than I'd like) that I was mistaken about an opportunity or a friendship. When that happens, it really throws me for a loop. I don't understand why anyone would waste time as a "friend" if they didn't have honorable intentions. What's the point? Who are these monsters? How can they sleep at night?

It's disappointing to discover someone isn't who they pretended to be. But, looking back on the situations, I can almost always find at least a few red flags that I overlooked in an effort to give people the benefit of the doubt. That's why I feel it's so important to teach kids that they should follow their instincts. When we're kids, our instincts are very strong. We are conditioned by well-meaning loved ones, teachers, and society to override our gut feelings and (at least in my case) over-intellectualize situations, removing the emotion and the insight it provides.

I'm getting better at feeling and listening to my intuition. When something feels wrong or off to me, I'm much less likely to question myself about it. Instead, I'm more likely to listen and get away from whatever or whoever is triggering the danger signals in my body. Listening to myself in this way builds my relationship and trust with myself and keeps me out of harm's way.

Questioning my instinct and overthinking it is what gets me into trouble sometimes. If I hesitate to honor my feelings, then I end up mired in an awkward situation later from which I have to extricate myself. This happens to all of us, so be gentle with yourself when you realize that it's happened to you. Just acknowledge the reality of the situation and remove yourself from it as quickly and as gracefully as you can. Whenever possible, seek to make choices that create more peacefulness in your life; that's almost always the best choice.

True Alchemy: Turning Trauma into Gold

Sometimes bad things happen to good people. Actually, this is just life and bad things happen to everyone, no matter how honorable you are. This sounds so obvious, but I still find myself getting caught up in faulty thinking about this sometimes. I wanted to believe that if you were a good person and did good in the world, that nothing bad would ever happen to you. Wouldn't that be wonderful? I guess I was taking the message of *The Secret* a little too far and unintentionally blaming the victim (myself) for everything that happened around me as if I was somehow responsible for it and could magically fix it. Turns out, that's not true. Sometimes bad things just happen and there's nothing you could've done to prevent it or make it better in that moment. It's up to you to alchemize the negative experience into something positive after the fact. I'll give you an example from my own life that I rarely share.

When I was a freshman in college, I came back to visit my family in my hometown for Thanksgiving. I had just turned 18 and my sister was 16. We decided to go to a friend's house for a party Friday evening on the day after Thanksgiving. It was just starting to get dark, and we were driving my sister's 1985 used, gold Chevy Cavalier down the country back roads we had driven countless times before.

Just before 6 p.m., as we were listening to one of our favorite songs on the cassette player and making our way around a steep turn, a single oncoming car seemed to be coming into our lane. Julie asked me if I thought they were going to hit us and, in that instant, I said "no." I was wrong.

Suddenly, there was a crash of excruciatingly loud metal-on-metal and spinning. The cassette player stopped for a moment and then continued playing the song we had been singing moments before the impact. I saw the headlights of the oncoming car and closed my eyes as it sped closer. When I opened them a second later, I saw the windshield had shattered. I must've passed out then because I awakened to my little sister feverishly patting me on the face in a panic and begging me to wake up. Upon waking, the first thing I did was eject the cassette tape to stop the happy music from playing.

The car had been driving over 40 miles per hour on that country road, which wouldn't have been safe under any condition, but especially when the driver was heavily intoxicated. We tried to open Julie's door, but discovered that the front of the car had been enveloped into the back seat. The dashboard was up on my knees, which bled through my ripped tights. I could barely move from the impact, and my sister was trying to kick out the shattered windshield to get out of the car. Eventually, I was able to get my door open, and we climbed out of the wreckage.

It was several minutes before the ambulance arrived. Luckily, the residents of a nearby house heard the collision and came running out to help. They escorted us from the car. When we saw the other vehicle, we saw an older man slumped over the steering wheel with blood running out of his nose and down his face. We instinctively ran over to him, but the family that was helping us held us back. I still remember the look of the guy sitting there mumbling. The father from the house told us to stay away from him, that he could "smell the alcohol" from where we were standing. That was the first time I realized that we had been hit by a drunk driver.

The family took us down their long driveway into their home and allowed us to use their phone to call our mom. We lived less than two miles from where the accident had happened. My mom got there before the rescue team and was relieved that we were okay. We were beaten up pretty badly but had been incredibly lucky to survive a head-on collision. When the police and ambulance arrived, one of the officers was investigating the wreckage of our car and said that we were lucky to be alive, that most people wouldn't have walked away from that accident.

When the emergency team strapped my sister onto a gurney, she refused to get into the ambulance if I didn't ride with her. They originally had wanted us each to ride in separate ambulances, but she had a fit. I'd never seen her like that before, so passionate about anything. Once they loaded us both into the ambulance and we were on our way to the hospital, she reached up to me and tugged a piece of my hair that often fell into my face and said, "if anything had ever happened to you." It was a beautiful moment because up until that time, we had been typical teenagers and not very close. Surviving that experience together bonded us in a new way.

The next day, my purse was missing, so we returned to the scene of the accident and found my personal belongings, including my wallet and my college ID, scattered all over the ditch and side of the road. We were very lucky that we didn't sustain greater injuries. We underwent a little physical therapy, and Julie had surgery to remove shrapnel from her arm. Years later, I had my spine examined, and the doctor determined I had permanent damage from whiplash at the base of my spine that should've been treated but wasn't. Beyond the physical experience, it was an emotionally traumatizing event. I was afraid to drive for a while and had to take time off from working because my legs, back, neck, and shoulders were out of alignment and caused me pain when standing for any length of time.

On top of that, we had to go to court and face the drunk driver who almost killed us. It was terrible because every time we got the letter for a court date, I would take time away from college and drive home for it, Julie would miss high school, and my mom would take the day off from work to sit and wait in the courtroom only to have the driver not show up. This went on for months and was a maddening waste of our time. It felt as if we'd never be able to move forward.

In the meantime, the wreckage of my sister's car was locked in a parking lot in the middle of our small town that we drove by almost daily.

My mom was very frustrated and made a giant sign that said, *This is what drunk drivers do to our children,* and posted it on the hood of the car so everyone would know that the accident was the result of a drunk driver. It came out later that the driver of the other car was a known alcoholic who drove drunk regularly after leaving one of his family member's homes. They actually knew he was drunk before he left and let him drive anyway, as they had done many times before.

The day we were in the courtroom and he finally showed up to take accountability for his actions (almost a year later), the man's son was there. I was surprised to discover that it was a boy from my high school who had been in my grade. I didn't know him personally, but we attended a small school and everyone knew of just about everyone else. I felt so bad for him and the situation that he was dealing with. Finally, the case was settled, and the car was removed from the pen in town. We were able to go back to our lives and focus on the future.

For years, I wondered why that accident had happened to us. Of course, when people hear there was an accident involving a drunk driver and teenagers, they usually assume it was the teenagers at fault. That wasn't the case for us. I couldn't listen to the song that was playing when it happened for several years because it would bring back the memory of that terrible night. It was the first car accident I'd ever been in, and it scared me. I decided that night that I would never drink and drive, would never get into a car with someone who had been drinking, and would stop anyone I suspected had been drinking from driving as well.

Most people are lucky enough to have never been in an accident like that, to never have almost lost someone they loved to someone else's inability to control their impulses and make conscientious decisions. I felt like it was my responsibility to educate fellow students about the hazards of their drinking habits. You can imagine how fun and popular this made me when I went back to college, but I didn't care. I was determined to mine this incident for gold, to alchemize the trauma into something positive that could make a difference. Because of that experience, I valued my sister, my life, and my responsibility on the road more than ever before.

Animal Lover

I've always loved animals. Dogs, cats, dolphins, cows, giraffes, monkeys, etc. I like them all. Everyone I knew growing up ate meat. It was almost heresy for someone to turn down a meal, especially if it was because it was made from an animal. I felt guilty eating animals ever since I was old enough to realize where food came from. Growing up in a rural area surrounded by farms, I felt a little too close for comfort.

While I was in grad school, I made a proposal to my grad program to pay for my admittance to an American Institute of Graphic Arts (AIGA) conference that was taking place in Washington, D.C. I was studying ecommerce and marketing and wanted to improve my design skills. The conference seemed like an awesome way for me to meet other designers and learn new techniques. I was thrilled when they approved my request.

During the conference, I heard many great speakers talk about the inspiration behind their art. One of the speakers was Sue Coe who called herself a graphic witness. She was showcasing her art that was inspired by slaughterhouses. She wasn't a vegetarian and wasn't pushing a particular agenda (she was wearing a leather coat). She was just showing what she saw and talking about the ways it affected her and her art. I thought it was interesting and then headed off to lunch. I ate alone in the hotel restaurant and ordered a fried chicken salad, something I'd eaten many times before in other restaurants. When my food came, I couldn't help but consider the information I had just received. I thought about how sad it was that an animal had to be killed in order for me to eat lunch in a fancy hotel. It really disturbed me that my actions weren't in alignment with my beliefs, and I found it difficult to eat.

On that day, March 22, 2003, I made the decision that I was going to be vegetarian. It felt like the right thing for me to do to assuage all the ill feelings I had about eating animals. When I got home from the conference, I began reading books and articles about the intelligence of animals and the impact that breeding and raising animals to be consumed has on our planet. All of these things reinforced my decision, but it wasn't easy.

Back then, there were not nearly as many vegetarian options on menus or in grocery stores. Of course, there were always salads, but I wanted to eat more substantial foods than salad. I made the choice every day when I woke up and chose foods in alignment with my decision all day long. It became second nature to look for the foods I could eat and not make a big deal about it to anyone else.

An unexpected benefit of replacing meat in my diet was that my physical health dramatically improved. Before I made that decision, I was suffering with a condition called gastroesophageal reflux disease (GERD) where I was experiencing debilitating heartburn after every meal. I was on a prescription that had limited impact and was considering having surgery in hopes of reducing the pain and damage it was causing to my esophagus. Within 24 hours of no longer eating meat, something miraculous happened—the GERD mysteriously disappeared! It was completely gone, and I haven't had heartburn in the 17 years since. It was a miracle that saved me tons of money in prescriptions and tripled my productivity because I was no longer spending three or more hours in bed per day dealing with the pain.

I don't know what it was about meat that was causing my body to react in that way. I never suspected rationally that it was what I was eating. I know that all bodies are different and need varying combinations of foods. I respect other people's choices to fuel their bodies as it feels right to them. Intuitively, I think I always knew that a more plant-based diet was best for me, and my feelings were trying to tell me for years. When I finally listened, it changed my life for the better.

The hardest part of making the choice of becoming vegetarian was explaining or defending it to people who seemed to take it personally that I was eating differently than them. In the first few months, I would take my time explaining my decision to them in hopes of gaining their acceptance. But I found that these words were almost always wasted because most people didn't care. They just wanted to make me wrong so they would feel justified in their own choices. Now that there's so much more awareness of plant-based diets, I get more high-fives than challenging questions.

About six months after becoming vegetarian, I decided to add seafood back into my diet and transition into becoming a pescatarian. I've continued to have high energy, clear thinking, and satisfaction with that choice. It made it much easier for me to eat in restaurants and increased my enjoyment of my meals.

Once I learned the details of what goes on with the meat before it reached my plate, I no longer had to fight any feelings of missing out. Even if I were starving, I would never consider eating a muddy shoe, and that's how I feel about eating meat. It just doesn't process in my mind as an option. If others want to discover more about it for themselves, there's plenty of information available in books and online. I'm at peace with my choice and allow others the grace to make their own choice. I have compassion and understanding for others' choices and am not interested in trying to convert anyone to my point of view.

Only you can decide what's right for your body. Hearing Sue Coe speak was the push I needed to make more mindful choices about my diet and to do more good for animals. You just never know where inspiration will come from and where it might lead you. In my case, changing my mindset and making choices that aligned with my beliefs dramatically improved my health and well-being. That's not one of the benefits I anticipated from attending a graphic design conference, but I'll gladly receive it!

People Are People Wherever You Go

My mom has a saying that she uses a lot that goes, "People are people wherever you go." I've learned that it's true. She usually shares this bit of wisdom when I'm telling her about an experience in which someone has done something crazy or disappointed me in some way. It is reassuring to know that the random weird things that happen to you aren't personal, it's just the way some people are.

Late people are late for almost everything, not just lunch with you. Irresponsible people are irresponsible almost all the time, not just with the project you gave them. Bitter people are bitter a lot of the time and nothing you say or do can truly change them. Grumpy people are grumpy. Greedy people are greedy. Happy people are happy. You get the idea. Try it on and see if it makes a difference in your own life. And, work hard to be one of the few happy, on-time, trustworthy, hardworking, generous, and joyful people in the world!

Peace in Action

1. What are you willing to let go of in order to create the time, space, money, and energy to make your dreams come true?
2. What are your energy drains and how quickly can they be removed?
3. Who do you need to forgive in order to move forward with your best life?
4. Stop List – "Hell No's" – What are you committed to no longer doing?
5. Priority List – "Hell Yeses" – What are you committed to doing to create your dream life?
6. What does your current environment (home, workplace, inbox, social media profiles, calendar, etc.) say about you?
7. What do you want your environment to be like? (Describe how it looks and feels and what it enables you to do.)
8. What is one element you can add to your environment that will make your heart smile? (For example: fresh-cut flowers in a vibrant color on your desk, a beautiful new purse, a framed photo of your family on vacation in your bedroom.)
9. What actions will you take to create peace and calm in your environment?

Peace on Social Media

Pinterest is my favorite social media platform to encourage Peace. Unlike the other popular social media tools, I find Pinterest to be more self-driven and less reliant on interactions with others. I use Pinterest as a personal, virtual vision board with the goals and adventures I hope to have in the future. I search by keyword and collect the images I enjoy the most. I personally don't really interact with others on the platform other than following accounts that consistently share images that I like. I only use it on my Mac or my laptop where I can fully enjoy the beauty of the images. For that reason, Pinterest is much lower-maintenance and more relaxing than the other platforms for me.

Let's Connect on Pinterest

https://www.Pinterest.com/SheriFink
https://www.Pinterest.com/SheriFink/Whimsical-World/

PASSION   PEACE   POWER   PROSPERITY   PANACHE

POWER

You owe it to yourself to become everything
you ever dreamed of becoming.

When I feel powerful, I feel that my voice has value, my choices matter, and my actions can make a difference. For many years, I was afraid to stand fully in my power. It was as if admitting that I was powerful would force me to take responsibility for all of the things I didn't like in my life, and I wanted to believe that those things were not my fault. The problem is that lack of accountability keeps us stuck as victims in our lives. It makes us a passive actor following a script instead of the writer and director who controls the narrative. We are all capable of great things. We can choose to embrace our power and use it to make a difference and to empower others to go for their dreams as well.

Accountability and Alchemy

When we take full accountability for our lives, we alchemize seemingly negative occurrences into opportunities. We stand in our power and take action to get the results we want while letting go of the need to control the outcome.

Living Beyond Your Comfort Zone

It's hard to do the things that make us feel uncomfortable. But I've found that pushing through the discomfort and doing them anyway enables me not to be frozen in pursuit of my goals. It also makes it easier to move out of your comfort zone in the future. It's like working out at the gym. Strength training a muscle is very difficult at first. Over time, with consistency, we get stronger and can use progressively heavier weights. The same is true for me when I'm afraid to say "no" or to ask what may be perceived as a "stupid" question. The more I'm aligned with my values and my vision for my life, the better I'm able to do the hard thing and continue moving forward to bring that vision to life.

I still have to encourage myself with positive self-talk and celebrate the fact that I did the hard thing regardless of the outcome. As long as I do my part by following my inspirations and consistently take action (not waiting until the stars align and I'm in the mood), I find that circumstances and conditions align in better ways than I could've imagined. And I have a pretty vivid imagination!

Don't Let Other People's Limitations Limit You

Your life is so precious. Don't waste it seeking other people's approval or permission to pursue your dreams. Most people mean well when they tell you that your dream isn't possible. Every human has experienced some level of disappointment in their lives. Some people let disappointment define them and misguidedly want to protect you from the same disease. What they don't know is that the cure for disappointment is to persist in the direction of your dreams. No one knows what you're truly capable of—not even you! So, keep your vision alive and continue taking action and appreciating the journey along the way. I'm living proof that everything is possible when you keep dreaming, growing, and striving no matter what "they" say.

Authentic Friendship

When you truly honor yourself and your feelings, you don't need them to be accepted or validated by anyone else. When you are authentic and real, you don't need to impress others. You don't need to brag or prove your worth in any way. You're just yourself, and you stand quietly, confidently, and comfortably in your power.

You don't have to settle for fake friends who don't really care about you. I think it's important to have standards, a personal code of ethics, that guides your behavior. I don't understand people who don't. It's a waste of time to try to comprehend people who don't care about you. How much time are they investing trying to understand you? Your life is too precious to leave to chance with aimless, mediocre, or self-serving people who would rather use you than love you.

Plan B: Bee in a Bonnet

It can be frustrating when people or organizations drop the ball and don't do what they say they will. In the past, I blindly trusted people to the extent that if they said they'd do something, I believed them and went along my merry way. The only problem was that deadlines were flying by with no deliverables or apologies letting me know to expect a change in delivery date. That continually put me in a bad position, as I was depending on people to do their part. It made me feel angry and resentful that people weren't prioritizing their commitments to me and didn't seem to care about the inconvenience it caused me.

During a big transition time in my life, I experienced multiple people dropping balls unexpectedly all at once. It was very disappointing and frustrating. I developed a plan to decrease the chances of it happening in the future and to handle it when it did. I call it Plan B (short for "Bee in a Bonnet").

Here's how it works: I try to be as clear as possible in my communication and to crystalize what everyone has agreed to in writing (a legal contract for business matters and an email for personal ones). I create a reminder on my calendar to trigger me to follow-up when needed to make sure we're on track for doing whatever was agreed to by the date agreed. Typically, this friendly note reminds the person that I'm waiting for something and, realizing that I'm not going to forget about it, they get it done.

Sometimes asking for an update or an ETA in a friendly way is enough. For times when it's not, and I really need it done, I follow-up multiple times (like a bee in a bonnet, I just keep buzzing). The annoyance factor is generally enough for them to deliver. I also put clauses into my agreements that state if deliverables or payments are late, there's an extra fee. So, at least if I have to chase people, I'm being compensated for the inconvenience. I really hate chasing people. I have more important things to do and won't continue to work with anyone who disrespects my time.

I've had success with clarifying expectations upfront, keeping tabs on progress, and eliminating or replacing people who don't make it a priority to keep their word. I'm not a micro-manager, but I keep track of my projects because I have a lot going on in my life and I refuse to be a victim to other people's poor planning and lack of boundaries.

Plan B is so effective that my husband has started using it and has also gotten things accomplished with fewer headaches. All you have to do is act as if the outcome is 100% dependent on you. If you take 100% of the responsibility, you'll make sure that things are done, even when having to depend on other people.

One side note: this is most effective when you're kind but direct, not angry or mean. If I'm waiting for something from someone, and they want something from me, I will make sure to ask directly about the status of my project (e.g., "When will this be complete?"). I don't need a bunch of excuses. I need a date because I often have other elements of my projects that are contingent on their piece being delivered.

I don't pretend that everything's okay when it's not. I also don't overdramatize the situation. Sometimes if people understand why you need it (i.e., it's not arbitrary), they'll work harder to get it done. If you think this sounds like a lot of work, it is. But I've found that it's less work and lower stress than the alternative of being surprised and let down when commitments aren't kept.

Breaking Up Is Hard to Do

Confession: For most of my life, I was addicted to soda. I had two personal favorites that I found irresistible on any menu. If the restaurant I was dining in happened to not have those options, I would feel irritated and cheated of a positive experience with my meal. It sounds crazy as I'm writing it, but that's how I truly felt. The large companies had done such a fabulous job marketing their products to me and making them addictive, that I would actually favor certain restaurants that I knew carried the sodas I liked.

I didn't even think this was a problem until I found myself craving the beverages. If I hadn't had one in 24 hours, my cravings would be intense. If I had a bad day or something stressful going on, or even if I had a good day and wanted to celebrate, soda was always a part of that. I even bought them in bulk from a warehouse store so that I'd never run out at home. But I started to feel a little strange when I got such strong cravings.

It seemed like I couldn't go a single day without drinking a soda, and that sounded ridiculous to me. I started having challenges limiting myself to just one a day and planning and anticipating when I'd actually get to drink it.

All this made me feel bananas. Was soda that important to me? Was my life so lame that drinking a soda was the highlight of my day? As I became more mindful and did some research, I discovered that these beverages contain lots of chemicals that aren't good for my body. I calculated how much I was spending per month and per year on soda in restaurants, and I didn't like the total. I could think of much better uses for that money than blowing it in a restaurant on a drink. To top it all off, the number of calories I was consuming in a week just in sodas was mind-boggling. There were so many signs that I needed to quit my habit, but in a weird way, I was scared to let it go.

Drinking soda was something I looked forward to every day. I thought that the bubbles in the drinks complemented my food and made eating a more pleasurable experience. When I wasn't paying attention, I tried to push these thoughts away. But I got to the point that I couldn't overlook the downsides anymore. I had tried to quit before and would make it three days before giving up when my cravings became so strong that I let them take over.

I took a vacation to the Big Island in Hawaii to do research for my book, *The Little Seahorse*. It was a fantastic trip that culminated in my first helicopter ride. I was excited to see the erupting volcano and tour parts of the island that can't be seen from any other viewpoint. But when I got to the airport, I was distressed that I would have to get on a massive scale and weigh in. It makes sense that they weigh each person the day of the helicopter flight to make sure that the weight is balanced in the seating arrangements, but I was panicking. I had been on vacation all week and had been indulging in sodas every day, desserts every night, and delicious island foods while leaving my gym clothes at home.

It didn't matter that I was the smallest person on my flight. When I got weighed in, I felt extreme shame over the number on the scale (which

was embedded in the wall with a bright red digital read-out for all to see).
It upset me so much that I almost let it ruin my experience. Instead, I
told myself that things would be different when I got back to California. I
would no longer let my cravings dictate my life. And with that declaration,
I held my head up high and boarded the helicopter for a magnificent
experience.

When I got home, I hired a personal trainer to help me reach my
health and fitness goals. I had read lots of books but didn't know what to
actually do. So many people say that their method, formula, supplement,
procedure is the best. I wanted to achieve my goals naturally, without
having to ingest any special pills, powders, or potions. Upon starting to
work with my trainer, the first step was to keep a food journal for a week
and to share it with him. Wow! That was eye-opening. Not only was it
something I hated doing, I also hated reading it and sharing it with a fit
person.

Of course, one of the first things he said was to stop drinking sodas
completely. No diet soda, no soda replacement drinks, just no soda.
I knew it was coming, and I was ready after my trip, but it was still
extremely difficult. At the time, I lived with roommates who were not
watching their weight, guzzling sodas all the time. I didn't personally buy
them anymore, but they were constantly within my reach.

The first week I had to rely heavily on willpower and the fear of being
chastised if I didn't keep this commitment to myself. That was enough
to push me through the cravings and last me through the week. Once
I started the second week, I felt proud of how many days I had made
healthier choices and was motivated not to break my streak. After a while,
the cravings diminished and I only felt them in triggering environments
like my old favorite restaurants, baseball games, and barbecues.

For the first year, commercials, delivery trucks, and others indulging
in sodas nearby still stoked the temptation to go back into my old habit.
But over time, those diminished and now I don't even notice or care about

any of those former triggers. I'm very happy to share that it's been over eight years, and I haven't had any soda since the day I decided to quit it. I no longer have a desire for it.

If you find yourself drawn to a habit that you want to stop, it helps to connect with the reasons you want to let it go. Write down all the ways that the habit isn't serving you or the person you're becoming. Set up your environment for success. If your weakness is potato chips, then don't bring them into your home or your office. Don't give yourself a temptation that will test you in your weakest moments. There is hope. The freedom that you'll feel when you're no longer doing something that isn't the best for you, and the energy that frees up in your body and mind, are worth it. Also, drink lots of water. People give the advice all the time and I used to ignore it, but it really is the best thing you can drink and is the most useful for your body whether you're fighting cravings or keeping fit.

Priorities and Possibilities

The better we become about determining our top priorities and setting boundaries to protect them, the greater potential we'll have for achieving our dreams. Setting goals, creating the vision, and overcoming procrastination are vital at this stage in our blooming process.

Pushing Through

I think writing is one of the hardest internally focused careers one can choose. Sometimes it feels like you'll never have a new idea again and like it's impossible to even compose a Facebook post. Other times, you're overwhelmed with so many ideas that you can't possibly capture or take action on them all at once. Sometimes you're highly motivated and determined to sit down to write then get deflated that the inspiration you felt just moments before has evaporated. Even the most strong-willed writer can melt into a puddle of self-doubt after staring at the glow of the blank page on the screen for long enough.

As soon as I commit time on my schedule for writing, it seems like everyone and everything conspires to stop me from keeping that commitment to myself. That's when emergencies pop up that have to be dealt with right away and also take all day. (Can you relate?) That's the time that my husband cooks up deliciously distracting plans. That's when my sister calls me and needs my help. I'm happy to give my attention and time to them, especially when it conspires to help me procrastinate on my writing. Sometimes I have to put up a brick wall just to make progress on my book. If I don't, the time will pass and I will be left feeling like a failure because I didn't take the simple, but extremely difficult, action of actually writing my book.

Years ago, I imagined (hoped) that it would get easier with future books. I figured that if you were a successful writer who had authored a book already, writing the next one would be a breeze. By then surely, I would have the necessary skills and magical attention span to easily finish writing new books. But, I've actually found that the opposite is true for me. I know what to do, but have a harder time doing it with so many more demands on my time. It's a good problem to have, but a challenge nonetheless.

I'm hoping that sharing this repetitive difficulty with you will help you feel better about whatever goal you have in your life that is making you question yourself and requiring you to find new ways to push through. I'm living proof that it's possible. It's not easy (even though I wish it would be), but it's worth it in the long run. I love days that I make lots of progress (or even a little progress). I feel like a superhero just for achieving the goal. I want you to push through long enough to feel that way, too.

The Struggle Is Real

I have a travel journal that I take with me on trips. I pulled it out for our recent trip to Virginia for Christmas and discovered an entry I had written a few years earlier when I was attempting to write *The Little Unicorn*. I was surprised to discover that the frustration and mixed feelings I was experiencing with my current work in progress (this book) were almost identical to the way I felt back then. Almost every book that I've written (except the first one which was written before I realized I was writing a book) has been a difficult dance balancing my calendar enough to allow time for the words to flow, keeping my butt in my chair long enough to coax them from the universe through my body and onto the page, and keeping my inner-critic from ripping it all apart before it even begins to come together.

Once you finally get a first draft written, the hardest part begins—the dreaded editing. I know writers who relish the opportunity to rewrite their books over and over, each time enhancing the characters, stories, and subplots. I, on the other hand, hate it. It's like hearing your own voice on an audio recording or watching yourself on video—painful no matter how well you actually did. I heavily incentivize myself to get through various checkpoints in the editing process because I know it's a necessary evil.

After rewriting so many times that I use up all of my best ideas and phrases, the next step is to actually share those words with other people. I cringe at the thought of that phase as well. It's important to have beta readers test-read the book before it goes into professional editing. That way, you know if it's actually working with your target market. For a children's book, I'll ask people I know and trust who are parents of children who are the appropriate age for the book, elementary school teachers, people who run nonprofits that benefit young children, and grandparents. Based on their responses and honest feedback, I make tweaks to the book and send the polished version to my editor.

Handing the manuscript off to a professional editor isn't as scary once you know that the beta readers already liked it. A good editor will rework the story and your phrasing to bring out the best in your writing and the book. I even have her edit my book blurb (the paragraph on the back of the book that summarizes the story) and my author bio (the blurb about me on the back cover of the book).

Once the editing is done, the manuscript goes to the illustrator for sketches of the main characters and the cover. Working with an illustrator can be fun. It can also be a lot of work. It requires having a vision for your book and serving as an art director to guide the illustrations in the direction that aligns with what you have in mind for the final version. Throughout the process, you have to clearly articulate the changes you want and have to be willing to speak up when things aren't going the way you like. My goal is to always do it with dignity and grace and hopefully to build the relationship, even if many changes are needed.

Keeping a project on budget and on schedule is a big deal if you're an independent author like me. You want to release the book at the right time to give it the best chance for success and to keep the costs low enough to make a profit on the books you sell. My goal is always to make a return on my investment (ROI) within the first six months that my book is officially available. Sometimes I've been lucky enough to make it back in the first two to three months thanks to strong pre-sale orders. But it doesn't happen by accident.

Throughout the writing, editing, illustrating, and printing process, I'm thinking about the marketing of the book. I even start talking about the upcoming book in media interviews up to a year in advance. Hinting that the book is on the way can help get Fans excited for it, but I've learned not to mention it publicly unless I'm fully committed to the release and know for sure that it's going to happen.

To change a pattern and get different outcomes in our lives, we have to do something different, to remove a domino from the pattern to disrupt the destructive cycle. It's a mental and emotional game to condition ourselves to think and behave differently in order to create better results in our lives. Pushing through when things get difficult helps us finish things that matter and up-level our lives.

Make Art, Not Excuses

Artists have a need to create. You may not consider yourself to be an artist and you may not consider what you create to be art, but it is. If I go a week without putting a pen to paper, I feel a strange imbalance in my life, almost like a feeling of creative constipation where my mind gets foggy and I feel vaguely sad. It doesn't seem to matter what I write, whether it's journaling my thoughts, writing a handwritten letter, or actually writing a book. Taking the time to write cures the condition.

I have had the honor of helping a lot of aspiring authors through my mentoring program. Many of them have had an idea for a book inside them for years by the time they find me. Most of them don't consider themselves to be writers at all, but the book idea grows so big within them that it becomes too painful not to write it. Something miraculous happens when they finally get the story out of them—they feel almost transformed, like a heavy weight has been lifted, and they have hope of making that dream finally come true. It's a beautiful thing to watch as they liberate the story idea that's been trapped within and, in the process, liberate themselves.

If you're a creative person, a high achiever, or a person who has a lot of ideas, you must channel that energy in a positive way so that you don't live your life in regret and resentment that you didn't fully express yourself. Artists need to create. Thinkers need to think. Dancers need to dance. Give yourself a worthy goal to work toward in an arena you love. It doesn't need to impress anyone. It's just for your sanity and enjoyment. Choosing to ignore the impulse to create causes a backup in our life pipeline. It can only be cleared by having the courage to do the thing that we need to do, even when we've built up resistance to doing it.

When I go for several days without putting a pen to paper, I don't quite feel like myself. Something feels off about the world and my relationship to it. Once I sit down and journal, even for a few minutes, some kind of magical release valve is pressed in my soul and the world somehow seems brighter, despite the nature of my writing. I experience a tremendous relief.

Pent up creative energy needs a channel, a place to release. I find it's as true for children as it is for adults. If a child with creative or intellectual talents isn't properly stimulated and challenged, they'll often exhibit emotional or behavioral problems. When we keep our minds engaged with positive uses for our abilities, we feel happier, more self-expressed, and more fulfilled at every age.

Creative expression also brightens my mood. It's almost as if writing and journaling is the way I talk to myself. And when I do it, I feel like I'm being valued and fully heard, like my ideas, thoughts, and opinions really matter. Journaling also helps me process thoughts and emotions. I gain perspective and better insight into myself and the world by writing everything out. It defuses the emotions I have trapped in my thoughts and makes me feel better. You can try this with any kind of creative expression and see what feels best for you.

If you are a creative person (and most of us are, even if we don't realize it), your life will feel better if you allow yourself the time and space to create. It could be writing, painting, dancing, scrapbooking, crafting, designing, singing, woodworking, etc. Whatever it is, schedule dedicated time on your calendar to create and watch your well-being improve as a result of your "play time."

If you think you don't have the time, take an honest look at how you're spending your days. Most of us spend multiple hours a day watching television. Wouldn't it be worth sacrificing one to two hours of watching other people's creations to make something of your own? If you knew that investing one to two hours a week in your art would lead you to holding your story idea in your hands as your very own book a year later, would you do it? Not to mention the sense of satisfaction and accomplishment you'll experience along the way.

Overcoming Procrastination

Writing a book is hard. I'm prone to procrastination and focusing on everything else in order to avoid the inevitable pain (and joy) of actually writing. I typically get the inspiration to write something long before I have the time to do it. It's harder to pick it up later and have the same gusto to write it. The books that have been the most fun to write were written when inspiration was immediately present. Only two of my books unfolded under those miraculous circumstances. All others were written long after the initial surge of inspiration had faded and only hard work and dedication enabled me to push through my mental and emotional resistance to finish the first draft.

I love the early inspiration and the final product, everything in the middle of that process is difficult. I'd like to say it gets easier with each book I write. In some ways it does because you at least have an idea of what to expect along the way. But mostly it's just hard and I have to stay disciplined with myself to do it anyway.

Even though I've climbed that mountain before, the path continually shifts, gets overgrown, and never becomes an easy escalator to the top. Sometimes it feels like I'm crawling up the mountain, but progress is progress. The more steps I take each day, no matter how small, the quicker

I ascend and accomplish my goal of bringing a new book into the world. And that is a very fulfilling and worthwhile endeavor.

Sometimes I enjoy hiding out in my analytical mind. It's easier for me to focus on getting things checked off of a list than it is to do my creative work. I'm a very creatively adventurous person, but I'm more comfortable using the logical rational side of my brain. Or maybe I'm just more rewarded from that type of thinking and action taking. It's easier to go down my priority list for the day and do the action-oriented things, leaving my writing and other creative endeavors for "later," which will inevitably be postponed as something else always comes up. (Can you relate?)

From what I understand from writer friends, it's a common dilemma, but at least I'm getting something meaningful done. I can relate to not wanting to do whatever I perceive to be the hardest or most uncomfortable task, but those projects and actions are also the most rewarding. The wise choice is to create environments that enable a balance, at least over the long run, so that multiple goals can be achieved, and we feel fulfilled and happy about how we're investing our valuable time and energy.

Our lives are not infinite. We have an unknown amount of time on Earth to make a difference. I don't want to spend all of mine watching reruns and playing video games (although I enjoy doing both). I have important things to do, people to help, and dreams to make come true.

It's really a matter of remembering how precious life is and taking care of ourselves in order to maximize the ways we use our time. I want to spend mine creating something new and beautiful, having amazing experiences with people I love, being surrounded by beauty, going on fun adventures, and making a massive positive difference in the world. When I get myself aligned with my vision, I feel a surge of energy, and I become unstoppable. Those are the days when I accomplish the most and go to bed feeling the best. Like most humans, this is not my default daily experience. But, I'm working on developing my mindset and perfecting my schedule to create more of those magical days. The more there are, the better for me, for my family and friends, for my Fans, and for the world.

Focusing on only one aspect of life to the detriment of all others is not my goal. I want to grow and flourish in all aspects of my life. I may get there a little (or a lot) slower than someone who only cares about one thing, but when I get there, I'll know that I didn't take any shortcuts or do it at the expense of my family, my health, my integrity, or my authentic self. That will make the journey and the destination that much more rewarding for me.

Stand in Your Power

I've mentioned that establishing boundaries is important for peace of mind, but they are also vital in order to stand in your power and own your life. I used to be terrible at speaking my truth and saying "no." I didn't want to hurt people's feelings, so instead I hurt my own by not honoring my feelings and standing up for myself. Sometimes I just didn't know the right words. Now I'm much better at only saying "yes" to people, things, and opportunities that align with my values and my vision for my life. I understand now that although I have a heart that always wants to help, sometimes the best choice is to help myself by avoiding overcommitting myself when I should be doing things that propel me forward, and in doing so, help others as well.

Whenever I'm struggling with an issue in my life, it is almost always some variation on a poorly set, badly maintained, or completely violated boundary. It's difficult for people to respect our boundaries if we don't respect ourselves enough to articulate them clearly and reinforce them as needed. It's challenging at first if you've been socialized into trivializing your needs and feelings, but it gets easier with practice. Once you know your worth and value, it's easier to naturally stand up for yourself and your rights. Life is so much better when your relationships are mutually respectful.

Courage and Confidence

Most of the limitations we set on ourselves come from worrying about what other people will think of us. If we release the need to please others and the desire to make other people's feelings more important than our own, we can move forward with a powerful sense of confidence and courage to do what it takes to live our dreams.

What Matters Most

I used to think that other people's opinions of me were important. I would inadvertently give my power away every day to people in my environment, even complete strangers who happened to be standing in line near me in the grocery store. It was as if everyone's opinion of me mattered more than my own. It sounds crazy as I write it, but it's a true confession. I was painfully insecure and grew up comparing myself to the people around me (and never measuring up).

It didn't seem to make a difference how many jobs I excelled at, how many degrees I earned, or how many pounds I lost, I always felt like I was chasing an ideal version of me in my future, one that was absolutely perfect: fit, healthy, energetic, sexy body; thriving business and the bank account to go along with it; handsome husband who adores me and isn't afraid to show it; charming friends who inspire and encourage me; fun adventures throughout the world with people I love; big, beautiful home filled with treasures collected on my travels; awards and acknowledgements; gorgeous clothing and accessories; and the list goes on. It's not that I don't want these things now. I just realize that checking off this list is not what really matters.

What matters most is the person I'm being and the way I'm feeling as I'm living my life and pursuing my dreams. If I have perfect health and fitness but no purposeful career that I'm passionate about and no one to experience life with, it becomes pretty meaningless. I used to get hyper-focused on a single goal and let the others fall by the wayside as I made big strides toward the one dream. I found that wasn't very fulfilling either. I feel I'm living my best life when I'm calm, confident, and flexibly focused. It's more about cultivating the inner peace and fulfillment in my internal world and then following those feelings to create success in the external world. It doesn't matter how good you look if you don't feel good on the inside. I haven't met anyone who looks and feels good all the time, but I've learned a few things that work for me to increase the opportunities for those two internal and external worlds to align and create magic in my life.

When I take extraordinary care of myself, everything in life is a richer and more fulfilling experience. Even challenges are easier to weather when you're nurturing yourself in a healthy, sustainable way. I have no interest in quick results that vanish just as quickly as they came. I'm interested in making little changes that have big impact over time, like meditating each day, working out, and getting an extra hour of sleep.

I'm constantly experimenting with the elements and actions that create a productive day and a deeply satisfying life. My body is a construction zone where I'm working to build new muscles and sculpt a stronger physical self. My mind is an ocean I'm sailing in exploration of the depth and width of my soul and deepening my connection to the universe. Every day can be an exciting adventure when you're tweaking your routine and your activities to see what makes your soul absolutely sing.

When I think of the times in my life when I've felt powerful, it seems to be when I've felt the most accomplished. For example, some of my proudest accomplishments that made me feel powerful are:

1. Being the first person in my family to graduate from college with a bachelor's degree
2. Graduating with honors with my master's degree while working three jobs
3. Fulfilling my lifelong dream of moving to Southern California
4. Finally leaving my corporate job to become an entrepreneur
5. Publishing my first #1 best-selling book, *The Little Rose*

6. Walking away from toxic relationships with people who didn't have my best interests at heart
7. Publishing my first international best-selling romance novel, *Cake in Bed*, and celebrating the release with a red-carpet event in Beverly Hills
8. Meeting and marrying my soulmate, my husband Derek
9. Founding my company with the mission of helping children with their self-esteem
10. Becoming debt-free

Each of these achievements represent years of soul-searching, planning, working, and staying true to my authentic self. These really stand out to me as major turning points, creating freedom and opportunity in my life while leading me closer to my destiny. I'm so grateful that I focused on what really mattered, even when it was hard, even when I felt pulled in a million different directions, even when it would've been much easier, and even understandable, if I had given up.

Overcoming Fear and Anxiety

Why are we afraid to tell our stories? Why do we even care what others think? Why are there "Like" buttons on everything we buy, videos we watch, and personal photographs we share online? What difference does the opinion of misguided people matter when you're busy making your difference?

I believe the answer to all of these questions is some form of fear. Fear of what someone else will think, fear that we won't be accepted and loved, fear that we won't be able to handle rejection, fear that we won't be able to keep up with success, fear that we're going to somehow be let down if we get honest or get our hopes up. But what I've found is that fear is only big and imposing when you refuse to look at it.

When you purposefully avoid your fear instead of doing things that will bring you face-to-face with it, you allow it to expand to epic proportions and make it "okay" for yourself not to stretch and grow for fear of feeling afraid. When I think of it that way, it sounds like a pretty silly thing for us to do. The metaphorical monster under the bed is our own shadow that we're imagining to be something real.

I like the explanation of fear as: False Evidence Appearing Real. It's human nature to feel afraid of the unknown and to have a strong penchant for survival. But unlike generations ago when we could be eaten as lunch by a lion, we're getting stressed out just by the prospect of going to lunch. And we sometimes allow the fear of feeling uncomfortable, or out of our element, keep us from fully living our lives.

As someone who is a true introvert and tends to be fairly shy in social settings, I definitely missed many opportunities to make new friends, to connect with colleagues, and to possibly up-level my career because I felt incredibly awkward and didn't want to risk the discomfort of doing things socially. Even now, I have anxious thoughts about it but lovingly push myself beyond my cozy, insulated comfort zone.

Confession: I still get nervous before I go on stage whether I'm talking to a group of 20 kindergartners or 1,000 entrepreneurs. I get anxious before leading webinars, having business meetings, and going to lunch or dinner with colleagues. It used to really bother me that I was feeling uneasy even after doing these things hundreds of times over the years. I assumed that it would become easier and easier and, to a degree, it has, but I still have anxiety. I've learned to listen to myself and feel the feelings, even though it feels like the most natural response is to push them away and pretend they don't exist.

Once I accept that I'm feeling anxious, I can breathe more fully and be there for myself in my time of need. I also say a little silent prayer right before I start that helps me a lot: "Thank you for the opportunity to be a blessing to others. Please help whatever I'm meant to say come through me without my interference." Resetting the expectation that the information is going to flow through me to the audience helps to take my focus off of myself and stop being self-conscious about every word.

I remember taking speaker training that taught where to stand, how long to look at each person, how to make hand gestures, and what stories to tell as you're holding your book. I tried to learn those strategies but found that they felt fake to me. It was only when I let go of trying to look perfect, use the correct hand gestures, and make the proper eye contact that I began to actually enjoy speaking. Instead of overthinking my every move, I focus on the feelings I want the audience to feel and the impact I hope to have as a result of spending time with them in that moment.

Instead of following a script and feeling like a robot reading from a notecard, I have a general outline of what I want to cover that I've spent time developing prior to my speech. I use the outline (most often on a PowerPoint presentation) to guide me and prompt me to tell stories in the right order as I build up to the final take-away. It's like writing a symphony that inspires people to take action or to think of themselves or the world in a different way. A well-delivered speech is a work of art and that's what I strive for instead of focusing on the logistics of my delivery.

Once I started connecting with the emotion, I was truly connecting with the audience. I never know exactly what I'm going to say or which story is going to pop into my head in the moment, but that's part of the fun of presenting. If it was all scripted, it would be incredibly boring to deliver the same speech over and over.

Derek and I speak to thousands of students at schools throughout North America every year. We customize each presentation for the age and developmental level of the grades for which we're speaking, the curriculum and issues the school is dealing with, and the amount of time we have to deliver our talks. This is more work than just presenting the same thing again and again, but it's much more engaging and fun (even for us).

It's difficult at first to trust yourself enough to know that the right words will come to you at the right time, but you'll get there. I remember when I was first being interviewed about *The Little Rose* and how I would request the questions in advance so I could think about and write out my answers to feel fully prepared. Reading from prewritten responses might feel "safe," but it typically sounds dull and inauthentic to the listeners. I've learned over the years to vet the interviewer and program well and trust that they won't deviate from their format. When they ask questions that they know their unique listeners will want to hear answers to, I'll respond in the best way I can in the moment. It keeps interviews fresh and fun, especially when you're answering similar questions many times over and over.

Giving yourself the flexibility of responding in the way that feels right in the moment also saves you time and stress before and during the interview or conversation. You know your story better than anyone else. Trust that you'll get better and better telling it as time goes on.

Kindness Rocks

During my undergrad years in college, I attended many concerts. Experiencing live music was one of my favorite things to do. I saw a lot of bands and singers perform, and Garbage was my favorite. I admired the lead singer Shirley Manson. She was talented, strong, and badass; yet humble, vulnerable, and feminine—a rare combination for female singers in the mid-to-late '90s.

I'd seen them in concert multiple times around the DC area when I heard that they would be doing a signing at Tower Records to celebrate the release of their second album. On the day of the signing, I left extra early, got in the already-long line hours before they were scheduled to arrive, and fretted over whether or not they'd leave before I got to them.

As the line slowly reached their table, I could see them from between the shelves of CDs in the store. They looked so cool, and I was nervous. I could feel my anxiety rising as I practiced my mini-speech about how much I loved their music and how many times I had already seen them in concert, as the line inched closer and closer. When I finally got there, I couldn't say anything. I was totally overwhelmed and could only smile nervously. Shirley Manson said, "Hi, Beautiful!" and that just meant everything to me.

I admired her very much, and it made me feel like the hours in line were justified. I used to worry about meeting people I adored from a distance. I thought that maybe they wouldn't be as nice in person as I hoped they would. Thankfully, that's rarely been the case for me. She might've said it to everyone there that day, but that wouldn't have mattered to me. The fact that she called me "beautiful" at a time in my life when I was very unsure of myself and self-conscious of my appearance meant a lot to me.

Another moment when I met a celebrity that had a huge impact on me was when I had the pleasure of meeting Dean Koontz. The typically reclusive author was speaking in my town. My mom has been a big fan of his books for as long as I can remember. I was excited to get a few books signed for her. As with Garbage, there was a seemingly unending line of people ahead of me even though I had arrived a few hours early. I got in line holding my stack of freshly purchased books and hoped for the best.

Periodically, someone would come around and let us know that he would only be signing for an hour and that we were unlikely to get to meet him that day. Rattled but undeterred, I continued to wait. When I got into the room where I could actually see his signing table (and the still-very-long line ahead of me), I was told that he would be leaving in a few minutes. I figured I would just stay until the end, until I was sure that there was absolutely no chance.

To my surprise, he continued signing long past his scheduled time—several hours past. He was kind, humble, cordial, and friendly with everyone. He even took photos with each person, including a photo with someone's giant poodle! I didn't know that I was going to be a writer back then, but I told myself that if I ever had the pleasure of sitting on that side of the table, I would be kind like Dean Koontz.

Shirley Manson and Dean Koontz may never know the impact that meeting them had on me. I think about those experiences often when I have the pleasure of meeting Fans. I always want them to feel welcome and acknowledged. I love having actual conversations when there's time. I'm happy to take photos and to make it a magical moment for them and their children. I've had two experiences where meeting the author turned out to make me not want the books I had just purchased. I know sometimes people have a bad day or they get jaded with their popularity over time. I hope that I always treat people with the dignity, respect, and gratitude they deserve because without the Fans, none of us would have the privilege of sitting behind those signing tables.

Not Your Average Role Model

Being a role model is something I take very seriously. I want kids to see me for who I am, a multi-faceted woman who works hard, lives her dreams, and helps others while having fun and being feminine. I love dressing up and wearing costumes, but I'm mindful to not wear things that are too suggestive or make me feel uncomfortable. Sometimes it's quite difficult to find flirty outfits that don't cross the line. I only want to wear things that I'm proud of and that represent myself and my brand in a positive way.

There are times that I feel self-conscious and don't really want to be in the spotlight. Sometimes I feel like my clothes don't fit quite the way I want them to, and I'd rather sit down in the shadows and hide. But my mission on this planet is to empower kids to believe in themselves and go for their dreams. Maybe they feel self-conscious about their bodies, too, and are letting it hold them back. I want to make sure that I take every opportunity to make a positive difference, even when I don't really feel like it at first.

I think about what it would've meant to me to meet an actual author when I was a kid. I didn't meet a real author (Michael Chabon) until I was almost 30 years old! I wish I had met a children's author when I was younger. I dreamt of being a writer but didn't know for sure it was possible for me until I read the first three Harry Potter books as an adult.

I was in graduate school at the time and reading lots of books that were not fun. Textbooks and professional journals got me where I needed to go for my studies but weren't things that I truly enjoyed. Back then, the books that were repeatedly recommended to me were the literary fiction and contemporary romances that were topping the charts. I would diligently try to get into those books but felt that the main characters were so unrelatable. I didn't know anyone like those characters, and I felt like their struggles were relatively insignificant compared to the real challenges I was facing in my own life.

It wasn't until one fateful day when I was shopping in the clearance section of a Hallmark store in Fairfax, Virginia, and stumbled upon the first three Harry Potter books in paperback for one dollar each that my destiny started to change. From the moment I opened the first book, I didn't want to close it. I had a hard time even putting the book down to go to the bathroom. I couldn't remember feeling that way about a book before. The compulsive reading carried me through all three books in 24 hours. I don't even think I slept that night. I was unfamiliar with the Harry Potter brand and did some research online. I was enamored with J.K. Rowling's story and became a big fan of her and her books. I thought it would be incredible to create a magical world where readers could go to discover deeper truths about themselves.

From then on, I was hooked. I waited in line at midnight at bookstores when each of the next four books were released and read through them voraciously the moment I had them in my possession. I even traveled to London to tour the Warner Bros. Studio where they house many of the costumes, sets, and artifacts from the films. I was so moved when I walked through the Main Hall exhibit that I actually cried. The Harry Potter series got me into reading again, and I will forever be grateful to J.K. Rowling for her positive impact on my life and the lives of so many others who now love reading because of her art. I hope to one day get to thank her in person.

Remember Who You Are

Sometimes when we're going through difficult changes in our lives, it's easy to lose sight of who we are, even if we were the catalysts for the change. Years ago, when I was going through a divorce, I had to remind myself every day that I was more than the circumstances I was currently experiencing. The feelings of loss, fear, and instability were overwhelming at times. I wrote a poem to keep myself grounded in my truth so I could weather the storm and greet the sunshine on the other side. I called it *Remember Who You Are,* and I read it multiple times a day to reassure myself that I was going to make it through no matter what.

A few years later, I was approached by a producer who wanted to record an EP of me reading empowering messages that would be mixed with music and sold online to help people get inspired, love themselves, imagine their possibilities, and take action toward their dreams. I thought it was preposterous that I could record an album. I'm not a singer or a musician, and I know nothing about EPs or that industry. But he was convinced that it would be a hit and that it was a great opportunity for me to reach people in a new way. I politely declined, saying that I needed to work on my other projects. He was so confident in me that he told me that he'd wait for me, but not for long.

What he said to me wouldn't leave my mind. I started thinking about how cool it would be to reach people with an audio that they could listen to in the car, at the gym, and on the go. I loved the thought of having inspirational affirmation songs on my phone to play whenever I needed a boost. Then I remembered that poem I'd written years before, *Remember Who You Are.* I dug it out of the drawer and reread it. It was just as powerful for me, but it also felt very personal. I wasn't sure I wanted to share it so vulnerably with the world. But I was feeling brave and dared myself to send it to the producer. I thought once he read it, he would understand that I wasn't the right person for the project, and he would pass.

Instead, he became so excited about the potential that he asked me to record a total of five songs for the EP. He also gave me a very short turnaround time to get the raw recordings to him. Excited about the possibilities and feeling like this could be fun even though it was completely outside of my comfort zone, I put my other projects on hold for the week and set about writing and recording five songs. When I was done with the raw recordings, I sent them to him to work his magic. He combined them with sound, and we released the album shortly afterward. I was genuinely surprised when it topped the Spoken Word charts on Amazon, beating even Deepak Chopra's albums!

The producer was so pleased with the final results that he approached me about doing a dance version of the album the following year. It would be the same words mixed with new tracks to make them more upbeat, instead of mellow and relaxing like the original album. I reluctantly agreed, and the rest is history.

I had no idea when I wrote that very private poem of reassurance during one of the most difficult times in my life, that I would later be willing to openly share it with the world. I've discovered that we all go through experiences we'd rather forget, and by sharing the tools that helped us through, we heal faster and make a positive difference for others who are facing challenges as well. I'm grateful that the producer had a vision that was much bigger than anything I'd imagined for myself. Trusting his intuition ignited a desire in me to try something new. I learned so much through the process. I'm grateful that I did.

Expansion and Empowerment

To live our most fulfilling lives, we must embrace living in a state of expansion, learning, and growth. As we discover who we are and what we really want, we transform into better versions of ourselves—inspiring our environments to evolve along with us.

Seeking Versus Creating

I love learning new things and meeting inspiring people. I'm in my element when I attend business and personal development conferences. They have served as catalysts for major transformation in my personal and professional life. I understood firsthand the value of being in those educational, inspiring environments and using them in my own evolution.

Years ago, I found myself investing thousands of dollars a year to attend conferences (and sometimes the same one over and over, year after year). It was a smart investment for me at the time when I was getting my bearings as an entrepreneur and making big changes in my life.

As I continued to attend, I noticed some interesting things about the personal development industry. Even if the content was the same or similar to what I'd heard in the past, I was a different person than the last time I had attended and, each time, I discovered something new about myself. As long as you're open to it, you can have new discoveries no matter where you are, but a powerful positive atmosphere will escalate and amplify your transformation, if you allow it to.

Another thing I started to see is that my experience would vary depending on my fellow attendees. I always meet good people and often make new friends. Sometimes people are more open and committed to the process than others. It seems crazy to me to pay all of that money and then skip sessions or be incredibly skeptical and not fully participate. I quickly learned to look for and sit next to the people who seem to be having the time of their lives. Their enthusiasm was contagious, and they inevitably seemed to make the best long-term friends.

Some conferences are designed to inform, educate, and transform while others are designed to deliver sales pitches from the stage in a high-pressure sales atmosphere. The latter may offer some value, but the primary purpose of it is sales, and that changes the vibe of the event. Some of them even plant people in the audience to run to the back of the room to look like they're going to sign up for their services during their sales pitches! I couldn't believe what was happening when one speaker literally told an audience of 400 people that they were "morons" if they didn't sign up for his expensive program. That experience left a bad taste in my mouth, and I decided never to attend that type of event again.

I also noticed that a lot of people attend the same events year after year (like I did) but appeared to be in the same situations every time. It's as if they're attending for the pep rally, but never fully putting that information and energy to use by playing the game. I would be happy to see a familiar face in the crowd, and then, while catching up, would have an eerily similar conversation about their challenges as we'd had the year before and the year before that. After many déjà vu moments, I realized that there's a population of good people who somehow become personal development junkies, always investing in the conferences and programs while rarely implementing their learnings in their lives or careers. This shocks me. Why would you invest the time, money, and energy into an experience and not do whatever it took to get a return on your investment?

Having these realizations and taking action in my life led me from a place of seeking to the powerful place of creating. I still love to learn, get inspired, and meet motivational people, and I balance that with my desire to create. I have ideas and ambitions that deserve my time, energy, money, and attention. I'm pouring all of those investments into finding the right recipe to create my own extraordinary life and to build an empire that inspires. Attending educational events is important, but it's not nearly as important as respecting my own time and actually doing something with all I've learned.

I want to learn from the masters, whether through books, podcasts, in-person, or online, and I want to create something masterful of my own.

So many people have good intentions when they set out as seekers, but they end up being a cookie cutter version of someone they admired and learned from. I want to be my unique, authentic self and to create my own strategies based on what I've learned and what I've actually done in my life. I don't want my Fans to become copies of me, I want to inspire and empower them to be their best selves and express it in their own unique, authentic ways.

Just a Girl

Why do we women doubt ourselves so much? I think it starts when we're very young. While I was getting my nails done, I noticed something fascinating and disheartening. Three families came in at different times and the mother or grandmother would tell the young girl with her that she could pick any color. The girls' faces lit up at the prospect of choosing from the rainbow of colors on the wall. Each time, she would quickly choose one and the mother or grandmother would put down her choice by saying, "Oh, these are prettier" and handing her a different, smaller set of pre-approved colors to choose from; or say "That's too bright" and make her pick something else; or "That's green. You don't want green!"

Each time, the girls (I'm guessing ages five to nine) would look confused and doubtful before choosing something that would be met with approval. In one instance, the grandmother told the girl to pick a color for her. The little girl froze and didn't choose one, probably because she was afraid of picking the "wrong" color.

Why didn't they just let the little girls have the colors they wanted? I know the parents and grandparents meant well, but this is how society inadvertently conditions women to doubt ourselves and our choices. It's so easy to just let those vibrant little girls pick their own color and express their individuality in their nail polish.

Let's not allow society to limit our choices. And, for the record, the salon didn't have the color I dreamt up, so I had them make a new sparkly purple one for me, a color I'm calling "Intergalactic Magic." Cheers to our girls (and boys) getting to choose their own magic!

Representation Matters

I've learned a lot over the past decade working with young children. I used to think that kids could easily see themselves doing whatever it was that the main character in a book or a movie was doing, and that they could empathize enough to relate no matter what that main character looked like. And maybe that's true to an extent.

Even looking back at my own childhood, I always wanted to see the one girl who was usually in the lineup of characters in a series. Even though I could relate to the male characters, it was more fun to play She-Ra than it was to be a supporting character in He-Man. I was much more fascinated with Smurfette than any of the other Smurfs simply because she was a girl like me.

Fast forward to the past few years, and I've had multiple examples of why my early assumptions were wrong and why representation matters so much. Here are a few to illuminate how I came to this conclusion:

I was tagged in a heartfelt Facebook post written by another writer who shared that he writes almost every day at home in front of his kids. But it wasn't until he took his daughters to see me at the premiere event for my book, *The Little Seahorse,* that they started saying they wanted to be writers. I guess it didn't occur to them that girls could be writers like daddy, too, until they saw another girl doing it.

Another reminder of how important representation is came during one of our school visits following the release of the movie, *Star Wars: The Force Awakens.* Derek and I do presentations together for assemblies of hundreds of students at elementary schools during the school year. We start by showing pictures of ourselves when we were their age. Derek's photo shows him dressed as Luke Skywalker holding a lightsaber. He playfully asks the students who they think he was for Halloween and the answers are often hilarious. They guess things like Harry Potter, Darth Vader, etc. but my favorite answer was "a Jedi." He said, "That's right, I was a Jedi." And a little girl shouted out, "Nuh uh, Jedis are girls!" It cracked me up because she's right, based on her experience, Jedis are girls. But based on my experience, Jedis have mostly been boys up until recently. It was a valuable reminder that what we see often impacts what we think is possible.

One time, Derek and I spoke to 500 students at a very nice school in a wealthy area. Afterward, the principal came over and thanked us for our visit. I told her how much we enjoyed it. She said it was particularly moving for the students to see a husband-and-wife team of authors. I hadn't considered that to be so rare until she mentioned it. She went on to share that I was the first female author they'd had speak at their school in the 35 years that she's been there. I could hardly believe it. Children's publishing is the one industry that's 95% female, and it boggles my mind that they couldn't manage to find one female author in all those years. I was honored that Derek and I could serve as role models for the students that day.

Wait for Your Perfect Puzzle Piece

I have a confession: I enjoy working jigsaw puzzles. Laugh if you must, but I find them to be very relaxing and a great way for my problem-solving brain to take a break. Ideas flow through me when I make the time to do puzzles. While working one today, I came to the realization that relationships are like puzzles. There are many pieces that may look like they fit, but only the right one really does.

I spent many years in a relationship that looked like it fit but didn't feel quite right. I remember going to a friend's Christmas party in college. One of my quirkiest friends was there and he ended up meeting his future wife that night. He was so unique and awkward that he had never even been on a date before (we were only 19). But the moment the two of them met, everyone knew they were perfect together. Conversation was playful and easy between them. I remember feeling excited and hopeful for them while feeling a little lost and sad about my own relationship at the time.

Fast forward to a few years ago when I met the man who would become my husband. I had been dating for several years and had always been told, "When you know, you know." That advice used to frustrate me. As an overthinker who had never experienced true romantic love, I doubted it was possible to "just know." But, when I started dating my soulmate, all of that changed.

When Derek and I would go out with our friends or family members, every single one of them said afterward that they knew we were meant for each other. And, most importantly, we knew it, too. We are weird in the same special ways. He embraces the things about me that other guys tried to change or begrudgingly tolerated. I love things about him that he hasn't felt loved for before. We found the right piece in each other, and it's enabled me to relax, knowing that we're meant for each other, just like my quirky friend who's been happily married to his soulmate for over a decade now.

Once you're in a relationship with the right person, your puzzle pieces fit together, and you can easily create systems and processes together that empower your lives and help propel you toward achieving your mutual goals. For example, my husband and I have a shared Apple calendar so we can both see at a glance what we're doing individually and together. The calendar is color-coded (pink for my items, blue for Derek's, and green for shared items) and accessible on our phones, Macs, and laptops. When we book something, we immediately put it on the calendar and set a reminder so we're always on the same page personally and professionally.

If finding the right piece can happen for me, it can absolutely happen for you as well. I've learned not to try to force a puzzle piece to fit simply because it looks like it should or because I'm tired of working the puzzle. The more time we waste trying to make the wrong one fit, the more time goes by before we find the right one. When you discover you have the wrong piece, let it go and keep looking. The perfect piece is waiting for you somewhere in this big wide world—go find them!

The Ripple Effect

Growing up in a rural town has a lot of advantages, but because of its distance from the major cities, very few speakers and authors visited our school. As a matter of fact, I can't remember any except one motivational speaker named Dr. Willie Jolley. At the time, I had never heard of a "motivational speaker" or anyone who made a living telling stories on stage to inspire others. It was just an average assembly day until Dr. Jolley took the stage.

He was passionate, much more passionate than anyone I knew at the time. He spoke eloquently and vulnerably about his upbringing and the possibilities for our lives. I was mesmerized with him and his story. As a lifelong big dreamer, I was overwhelmed with joy when he talked about the benefits of hard work and dedication to your dreams.

Typically shy, I wasn't normally one to strike up a conversation with anyone, let alone a celebrity stranger. But I felt inspired and walked up to the stage to talk with Dr. Jolley after his speech. I told him that I really enjoyed his talk and thanked him for making the time to visit our school. Other students snickered and thought that I was wasting my time, but I felt like Dr. Jolley was a kindred spirit and there was no way I was going to miss the once-in-a-lifetime opportunity to meet someone who had indirectly supported my dreams.

He was very gracious and even wrote "Be great!" on an index card and signed his name for me. I kept that index card and never forgot the way he looked me in the eyes and told me that my dreams were possible, whatever they may be. Where I lived, I didn't have much of a cheering section for the audacious goals I was cooking up inside of me. So, it meant a lot that a grown-up who didn't have to be nice to me took a few minutes to chat with me.

Fast forward 20 years later and I was attending a Les Brown seminar. I signed up upon hearing that the amazing Les Brown would be speaking and didn't even bother to see who else might be there. I was just excited to hear one of the best motivational speakers of our time speak live. While I was returning to my seat after getting some water, I ran into Dr. Willie Jolley! I couldn't believe my luck.

Although I was nervous and certain that he wouldn't remember me, I walked up and told him who I was and the impact he had on me when I was in high school. He was gracious and kind, just like I remembered him, and was very excited to learn that I am writing books and doing inspirational speaking to empower people, especially kids. I was able to introduce my assistant to him and get a photo together. It was a beautiful, full-circle moment that I will always remember. Now that index card reminding me to "Be great!" means even more to me. So, never question that your kindness and your actions can have a ripple effect that can continue for many years and even generations to come.

It's Time to Soar

Sometimes when you're on a path of personal development, you grow in different directions from the people who are in your life. It's okay to evolve and to allow others to grow at their own speed. It's not a matter of becoming better or even of outgrowing people. I think of it more like I'm growing in a different direction. I've had this experience multiple times in my life, and especially over the past ten years as I've been on my entrepreneurial journey.

Sadly, some people will feel threatened when you change for the better. Maybe they liked the way you were before, when you had lower expectations for life and other people's behavior. Maybe they were more comfortable when the two of you would complain about anything and everything together. And now that you're trying to improve yourself, they've lost their venting buddy. Don't let other people's comfort and expectations keep you stuck. If you know that you're meant to change something in your life, get to work changing it. Get so busy doing the "right" things that you don't have time to do the "wrong" things anymore.

A wise friend of mine gave me some advice when I was considering resigning from a group that had once brought me great joy over multiple years but had been consistently feeling like a burden for several months. It was made up of other entrepreneurial business owners and leaders in different industries, and we were helping each other build our lives and businesses. For years, it was like magic. I felt a kinship with the members of the group even though we were located all over the world and only met over the phone every other week. We helped each other brainstorm, solve problems, and up-level our dreams.

It was awesome, until it wasn't anymore. It seemed like several members would come unprepared for our regular calls. Although they knew what to do, they weren't doing it anymore. They would present the same problem to the group over and over. We had already provided support for those problems and they hadn't taken any action yet. It was frustrating to feel that I was wasting my time rehashing the same suggestions they already had but weren't using. In contrast, several members of the group were playing at a whole new level and would present challenges that the other members couldn't fathom, choosing to not provide support out of inexperience.

In talking through these challenges one day, it came out that some members were jealous of the success of several others (including me) and felt that it was blocking them from fully participating at the level they had before. These were people who knew me from the very beginning of my author career. They knew how hard I worked and some of the obstacles I had overcome to get to where I was. We had all helped each other for so many years, but it didn't seem to matter. They couldn't get past their own limitations in order to see the opportunity they were throwing away. How could I trust people to advise me on my business when they were jealous of my success? I knew in that moment that it was time for me to leave the group. It was a difficult decision, but the right one for me even though I struggled with it.

My friend gave me some good counsel during that time. She said that it was as if we were all walking along hand-in-hand on the beach at the same speed. Then, I discovered that we all had wings and I excitedly tried to get everyone to start flying together. But some of us weren't ready for flying and denied that we even had wings. At first, I landed back on the beach and walked with them again. But, knowing that I could soar through the sky, I could no longer settle for walking. They resented me for choosing something different, even though I didn't want to leave them behind. Even in their jealousy, they didn't want to hold me back. So, I had a very uncomfortable conversation about the way I was feeling and resigned from the group.

I felt a huge relief when I hung up the phone. I had been honest and compassionate with them. I loved them each very much no matter how they were feeling and acting. It would've been unfair for me to remain a part of the group and resent being made to walk. It would've been unfair of them to pretend everything was okay when they were feeling the need to slow down. Within days after I resigned, the group decided to disband. I'm still friends with the members, although we don't talk nearly as often as we used to. I know in my heart that I made the right decision for me and for my growth.

Women Empowered

A few years ago, my friend told me that she was doing something on Saturdays that she found incredibly empowering and that she thought I would like as well. I didn't ask too many questions, just confirmed a Saturday that I was available a few weeks later and asked what to wear. She said comfortable workout clothes would be best. So, on the day we agreed upon, I showed up to the address wearing workout gear.

When I arrived, I was greeted at the front door of a jiu-jitsu academy and was welcomed into the locker room. I was surprised and uneasy when we walked out onto a giant mat with at least 30 other women wearing gis. Seeing them roll around on the floor in what looked like their pajamas made my inner introvert want to run and hide. But my friend reassured me that I would love it, so I committed to sticking it out through the entire session.

When one of the instructors demonstrated with me how difficult it would be to get someone off of me from a position on the ground and then showed me a simple technique to use leverage instead of strength to roll him off of me, I was hooked. I wanted to become a "ninja" and know how to survive in tough situations when faced with an opponent who was bigger and stronger than me. I not only stayed for the entire introductory session, I enrolled in the academy and eventually graduated from the Women Empowered program, earning my pink belt and dramatically increasing my level of calm and confidence in the world.

I traveled many places on my own when I was single. I didn't feel the need to hold off on taking a trip I really wanted to experience just because I hadn't met my special someone yet and none of my friends were available. I would just book the trip and go. I've been to cities abroad for weeks at a time where I didn't speak the language (well, I tried, but mostly relied on kindness and hand gestures), as well as places throughout the United States. I never felt as afraid in any of those places as I've occasionally felt walking in Los Angeles and in parts of Washington, D.C.

Getting trained in jiu-jitsu helped me feel more confident being in parking garages, walking down the sidewalk, and even just heading off potential conflict. Of course, there's the psychological component of allowing other humans to be that close to you during the training, the courage to allow yourself to be fully seen and teachable, and the gift of giving yourself the freedom to make mistakes and learn from them along the way. Beyond the stretching of those comfort zones, I also grew stronger physically, mentally, and emotionally. The repetition of the movements and the ability to stay calm and determine the best move based on the scenario really empowered me.

I was afraid when I began the program. Those women seemed so self-assured and confident, yet warm and welcoming to new people. Although I felt anxious, I quickly made friends with these radiant creatures and continued to try every week, sometimes twice a week depending on my travel schedule. Shortly after I began attending regularly, my friend who had originally invited me put her training on hold to pursue another goal. I never considered quitting just because she wouldn't be there. I was committed to the process and being around these wonderfully powerful, yet humbly confident people.

About a year and a half after I began my training, I finally graduated and received my pink belt. It was such an exciting day. I knew I had worked hard for it, visualized that moment many times before, and passed the test to earn it. I had a twinge of sadness that I didn't have any local friends or family who could make it to the ceremony. Most of my friends had family members there to cheer them on and take photos. I was alone, but my ninja sisters never let me feel that way. They cheered loudly when my name was called, took photos of me, and even invited me to lunch to celebrate with their families. Not only had I gained self-confidence and ninja skills, but I'd also made true friends.

The Biggest Lessons I Learned on the Mat:

1. The person who walks away is the one who wins. Just because you can technically win a fight thanks to your training, doesn't mean that you should always engage in one. It's actually better to take the high road and diffuse the situation if you can. If that doesn't work and the fight is brought to you, then defend yourself and submit your opponent with everything you've got.

2. If someone is trying to force you to go with them, don't go. Do whatever you have to not to acquiesce to their threats because whatever they're going to do, it'll be much worse if you're in a secluded area away from any potential help. That information alone could save lives. Tell every woman you know.

3. Another part of the training I hated during the practice, but found to be extremely valuable, is finding your voice and being powerful from the beginning. So, if someone is coming near you and it feels uncomfortable, speaking up and telling them to stop before they're

too close to you will help you discern from their reaction what their true intentions are. For example, if you're in a dark parking lot and a man approaches you asking what time it is, and you respond by turning around, fully facing him, and saying, "Stop," and he continues moving forward, you know this man has ill-intent. Someone who doesn't would stop and apologize for scaring you.

4. When you're doing a move in jiu-jitsu, you have to follow through. Your body and mind have to be 100% committed to finishing the move or your limbs will be limp and easy to overcome. But if you lock your arms at the elbow and fully carry out the move, you will be successful and free yourself from your opponent. I think actions in life are the same way. If you put half-hearted, doubtful energy into something, you'll get the same kind of results. But if you believe with all your heart and fully go for it, you'll be successful.

5. Practicing moves over and over helps them become reflexes. Repetition is the key. When I first started, I couldn't even remember the names of each of the moves, much less which ones to do based on the position of the opponent. But, with consistent practice over time, I started to just know what to do. It became much easier, but not before it was quite hard and confusing.

6. My instructor Eve Gracie taught me that it's smart to have certain rules for your life, like boundaries for what you will and won't tolerate or do no matter what. Most of us have some basic rules, like not killing anyone, but it's worth it to consider the types of boundaries we can put into place to help prevent the potential of being faced with a horrific situation. Here are a few of mine:
   a. Never have an alcoholic beverage and drive.
   b. Never get into a car with someone who's been drinking.
   c. Never allow myself to be alone in a bedroom or hotel room with any man who is not my husband, my father, or my child.
   d. Never stay in any environment or situation that gives me the creeps (follow my intuition—if something feels wrong, trust that it is wrong for me and leave immediately).

e. Never pretend not to notice suspicious behavior. Look right at it and address it in the moment. A boundary that's set early is easier to enforce and makes you a harder target.

f. Never accept drinks from a stranger.

g. Always charge my phone battery overnight and when in the car so that I have power when I need it.

h. Always stay with the group I came in with—don't allow myself to get isolated from my friends.

i. Always enforce healthy boundaries. Friends who don't care about your feelings aren't your real friends.

7. Another element of Gracie Academy that intrigued and inspired me was the couple who trained my class, Eve and Rener Gracie. They are both beautiful and immensely talented individuals who are deeply humble. When I first met them at that introductory session, Eve was visibly pregnant and was the most badass woman I'd ever seen. She was demonstrating the moves on how to ward off an attacker alongside her husband. It inspired me to see a powerful couple working together in life and business to make a positive difference for others. It aligned with my mission and my hope for my own life back when I was single. Getting to see them interact with each other with love, humor, grace, and respect every week was an added bonus for me.

I never thought I'd be one of those pajama-wearing wrestling people, but keeping my heart and my mind open enabled me to seize the opportunity for self-improvement, personal growth, and general badassery. I'm so grateful to my friend for inviting me that day and that I completed the training. Graduation day was a proud moment built from many smaller moments that alone felt insignificant, but together made a powerful difference in my mindset and my life.

Power in Action

1. In what areas of your life do you want to feel more powerful?
2. What could you do, change, or accept to feel more confident and empowered?
3. What could you do to empower others?
4. What processes or systems could you put in place to empower your life?
5. What do you want to outgrow or evolve from in order to achieve your dreams?

Power on Social Media

Twitter is my favorite social media platform to practice Power. Strategically searching hashtags enables you to have the most up-to-date news and information. The great thing about Twitter is that everyone has the power for their voice to be heard, and often times much faster than the traditional media can synthesize it all to report on it. Keeping on top of the latest news can help inform decisions you make in your life and business. Twitter can also be a great way to reach people who are typically unreachable. For these reasons, Twitter can empower you to be more knowledgeable, connected, and prepared in today's society.

Let's Connect on Twitter

https://Twitter.com/Sheri_Fink   @Sheri_Fink

https://Twitter.com/WhimsicalWorld7   @WhimsicalWorld7

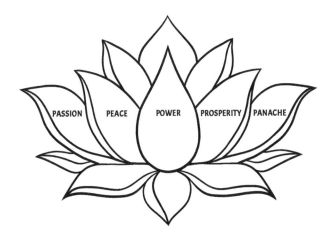

PASSION PEACE POWER PROSPERITY PANACHE

PROSPERITY

**Someone once told me not to bite off
more than I could chew. I said I'd rather choke
on greatness than nibble on mediocrity.**

When you feel prosperous, you have an abundance mentality that recognizes that you have good luck and you're going to play whatever cards you're dealt to the best of your ability. There's enough for everyone, and just because someone else is successful doesn't mean that you can't be as well. As a matter of fact, if she can do it, you can probably do it, too! It may be a combination of money, opportunities, or people, and it all contributes to you feeling more financially serene and grateful. But it doesn't happen by accident. Here are my favorite strategies for recognizing and attracting more prosperity into our lives.

Acceleration and Abundance

There are many forms of abundance that we can accelerate with clarity, creativity, and consciousness. When we're in alignment with our values and vision for our lives, abundance flows into us and through us easily and effortlessly.

Be a Dream Magnet

Don't chase your dreams—become a dream magnet. Have you ever wanted something or someone with such intensity that you gave off the stink of desperation so badly that even you were repulsed? Well, that energy of desperation seeps into everything you do and, because it comes from a place of scarcity, repels the very thing or person you want to attract. It's happened to the best of us at some point (or many points) on our journeys.

I find that I feel a lot better and achieve my goals faster when I work to become the best magnet for what I really want to attract. Becoming a magnet means acting and thinking in ways that align with the energy that you want to attract to yourself, serving as a beacon of light and love for all the juicy things and opportunities your heart desires. Focusing on yourself and improving your magnetism keeps you from feeling desperate because you're not depending on the external world to fulfill you. You're filling yourself up with love, fun, adventure, and excitement so that when the thing you want discovers you, it can't help but come to you. And, you're so busy having fun in the meantime that you're not hung up on when or how it's going to happen. You're living your life to the fullest and anything or anyone that you choose to allow into it has to match your powerful magnetic force.

If you want to attract love into your life, behave lovingly toward yourself. Say nice things that encourage you, give yourself the rest you deserve, buy yourself flowers every now and then, and glow with love from the inside out. When you truly love yourself wholeheartedly, people who don't love you will eventually drop out or drift out of your life. Don't be afraid. Recognizing your inherent value is a natural part of the process of evolving into the person you're meant to be. As you become more confident in yourself, you won't settle for people or behaviors that disrespect, belittle, or demean you anymore. As someone who's gone through this myself, I can tell you that resisting the urge to fall back into helplessness and codependency can be tough, but if you keep working at it and become stronger within yourself, you'll attract the most epic love you can imagine and you'll wonder how you settled for less all the years before.

If you want to attract generosity, be more generous with others. Even if you don't have the extra money to donate right now, you can still practice generosity of spirit. Maybe someone needs help and you know how to help them. Maybe you decide to brighten every room you walk into with your smile, positive attitude, and encouraging words. Maybe you declutter your home and donate your excess things to those who need them. Maybe you spend extra time listening to your friend who's going through a tough time. Maybe you give people more grace when they are late or make mistakes. There are many ways to be generous. Try a few and see if you attract more generosity and understanding into your life.

It's much easier to pull in the good than it is to push out the bad. Once you shift your focus from what's wrong with your situation to what you most want your situation to be, you can start taking action from a place of abundance and joy. You know what you want and so it's easier to discern when something comes along that's not it. And now that you have the tools to say "no," you won't waste your precious time on things, opportunities, and people who aren't a match for you anymore.

Always Use Your Stickers

Growing up, I anxiously awaited the arrival of the book club flyers and order forms at school. There was a series of books that contained stickers in them that I thought were the best things ever. I would pore over the order form, circle everything I wanted, and then try to convince my mom that I needed those books. Because we didn't have extra money in our budget and had more important priorities for our income, the answer was often "no." I would try to understand but would feel disappointed when the books were delivered to my classmates and I went home without one.

Every now and then, my mom would say "yes," and I'd be allowed to pick out one inexpensive book. I always gravitated toward those sticker books because they had a long story, fun illustrations, and stickers. I came across a handful of these books from my childhood when I was moving a few years ago. I remembered how excited I was to have them and how I would stare at those beautiful, colorful stickers.

I also remembered how much cognitive dissonance I had about them. On the one hand, I desperately wanted to use those stickers to decorate my school binder, my sticker book, and my bedroom. But on the other hand, it felt frivolous to use the stickers and then not be able to look at them in my special books again. So, I fought my impulse to use the stickers. When I flipped through the books as an adult, I looked at all of those perfect little stickers still on their sheets, and I cried.

As a kid, the books felt priceless to me although, upon closer inspection, they cost less than two dollars each. I was "saving" my stickers to preserve books that cost less than half a cup of coffee. Some of the books even had two of each sticker so you had one you could give and one you could keep. I was so afraid of regretting how I used them that I denied myself the pleasure of using a sticker for what it was meant for, sticking onto something to make you smile. And that made me feel sad for the little girl inside of me who never got to use her stickers in a way that brought her joy.

Never again. I used all of the stickers in those books that day, sticking them onto my grown-up notebooks and journals. I vowed moving forward to always use my stickers in life. What "stickers" do you have in your life? Are there special things in your life that you're not using because you don't know if what you want to do with them is "special" enough? In what ways are you denying yourself the pleasure of enjoying something you own? What could you do this week to reignite that enjoyment in your life?

Creating and Cultivating

The Percolating Lot

Early in my career, I promised my Fans a book called *The Little Unicorn*. When I went to write that story, I had so much trouble. I felt inspired at the time to write a romance novel called *Cake in Bed*. Even though I was putting the romance on hold to finish *The Little Unicorn,* I felt completely blocked and couldn't get the story where I wanted it to be. I could've released it as it was, but I never release any book that I don't feel proud of. While I was feeling frustrated about not being able to work it out, I called my mom and she suggested that I simply put the children's book on hold and write the romance novel. My mom is full of sage wisdom, but I thought she had lost her mind. I couldn't imagine not delivering on the book that I had promised. She reminded me that no one would suffer if my new children's book wasn't released on time.

After I thought about it, I realized that she was right. I could set that story aside for the time being so I could be free to focus on the romance novel I was having fun fantasizing about. So, I let my Fans know that I was putting the unicorn book on hold. Even though I felt like I was letting them down, no one died so it was okay. I put it in what I call the "percolating lot." When I worked in the corporate world, people would say they'd put an idea in the "parking lot" when they didn't really want to do it or didn't have the bandwidth to do it at the moment. I found that ideas and projects seemed to go to the parking lot to die. So, in my business when I want to save an idea to explore later, I put it on a list of percolating lot ideas to percolate and build steam for the future.

I reassured myself that my book idea would be safe there. Then I focused my energy on writing the story my heart really wanted to tell at that time. *Cake in Bed* debuted a year later and went on to become an international best seller. I still receive Fan mail from women who love that book, and I'm glad that I took my mom's advice and wrote it.

Fast forward a few years later and my husband asked me what my biggest writing regret was. I thought for a moment and then shared that I had started writing a unicorn book that I never finished and always wanted to. He encouraged me to pull it out of the drawer and finish it. I reread my draft and ended up starting over from scratch. When I finally had a story I was proud of, I released the book and it became my best-selling book ever. It's definitely better than it would've been if I had rushed to release it years ago. It's the book that I'm the proudest of because it was the hardest to write and had the longest journey to being published. The best part was being able to tell my Fans that I finally did it!

What to Do When You Feel Stuck

Have you tried a lot of these strategies and still don't seem to be making the traction you'd like? Sometimes we have to take new actions to shift our energy and our perceptions. Whenever I'm at a point where things seem to be plateauing, I have several things I do that seem to magically shift my situation:

Donate money. I'm not sure why this works, but it seems to make a difference. Choose a cause or multiple causes and give what you can. Give a little bit more than you're comfortable with. When we donate money, we're sending out the signal to the universe that we are abundant, generous, and kind. Donating your time is also great, but donating money is what really moves the needle. It's scary at first if you don't have a lot of extra money laying around, but the positive feeling you get from giving even a modest amount is worth it. Those vibes attract more money and abundance back to us.

I did an experiment once where I vowed to give money to anyone who asked for 30 days. For 30 consecutive days, I kept extra cash in my wallet and would give some to anyone who I saw holding a sign asking for money, who sent me a donation request online, who posted about a charity on social media, who had a tip jar in my view, and who could benefit from my help.

It was really liberating to give myself permission to give. I felt wealthy, generous, kind, and happy. I didn't worry myself with whether or not the person really needed it, what they would spend it on, or if one cause was better than another. I simply gave what felt right in the moment. Sometimes that was a dollar. Sometimes it was a lot more. The recipients were almost always overjoyed and looked me right in the eyes with a big thank you or God bless you. I received their gratitude and smiled back. And, in the rare case where they didn't seem grateful, I didn't bother thinking more about it. I did what I set out to do, and I spread good in the world, whether they acknowledged it or not didn't matter. Give this a try and see how it changes you and your dream magnetism.

Declutter your environment. When energy seems to be stuck and I feel like I'm not making any progress, another strategy I use is giving or throwing things away. We all collect things that we don't ultimately need at some point in our lives. As someone who used to gleefully accept any free thing I was offered (now I'm blushing), I accumulated a lot of stuff that wasn't necessary in my home. I like to purge things in groups of 10, so I will tell myself to let go of (either recycle, donate, or throw away, whichever feels the most appropriate for each item) at least 10, 20, or, if I really want to shift my mojo, 30 things.

The items don't have to be large, valuable, or important (but you get bonus points if they are any of those things). The point is to shift your energy from a place of scarcity and lack to a place of abundance and generosity. Showing the universe that you trust that you can live without these things (and without feeling the need to immediately fill the void with more junk), sends out a powerful signal that you're ready and open for more money, opportunities, and abundance in your life. It also enhances your environment and gives you more space for awesomeness to enter, and who doesn't want that?

Do something new. It's easy to get caught in our day-to-day routine and do the same things day-in and day-out. We get up at the same time every day, eat the same breakfast, do the same workout, drive the same route to work, eat lunch at the same time, talk to the same people, etc.

Before long, you can do it all without thinking, which is efficient, but not the best way to attract living the life of your dreams.

Break out of the cycle (or just take a break from the cycle) by doing something you've never done before. Maybe it's taking a class one weekend. Maybe it's driving a different route to work. Maybe it's inviting a friend to join you for your usually solo lunch. Maybe it's trying a new restaurant or a new cuisine. Maybe it's watching the sunset. The point is to do something that feels different and awakens you from your routine. There's nothing wrong with having a routine. It's when you start to lose energy that it becomes a rut. Do something new and different to enliven your senses, make you feel present and alive, and attract more magic into your life.

Dedicate your dream. Think about something or someone you really love, someone who's made a powerfully positive difference in your life. Feel the joy and gratitude you have for the impactful actions they took and the long-term ripple effect they've had on you and your loved ones. Declare that your journey to achieving your big dream is dedicated to them. This not only honors someone who has made a difference, it elevates your dream with new energy associated with the gratitude you feel for them. This will enliven you to continue making progress and to associate your actions with honor and appreciation.

Writing a book is hard work. It takes focused commitment over a long period of time to write, publish, and market a book to reach the right audience. Dedicating each book to someone I love enables me to associate that project with them. It makes it easier for me to keep going when times get tough and I feel like giving up. When I think of them and what they've done, I'm able to associate the gratitude I feel for them with the book that I'm writing, and that gives me more motivation to finish the work at hand.

Your project may be something completely different than a book, but the process and the impact is the same. Maybe you're building a barn. Maybe you're learning a dance. Maybe you're earning a degree. Maybe you're starting a family. Maybe you're interviewing for a new job.

Maybe you're becoming debt-free. Whatever it is, dedicate your effort to someone and get reenergized to make that big, juicy dream come true.

Trust Divine Timing

You know how it feels when you want something to happen so badly and it feels like it's taking forever? Many times, when I feel that way (mostly because I'm a big dreamer who's fairly impatient), I have to remind myself that I've already put in my request to the universe (by setting my goal, visualizing its achievement, and taking action on my inspirations). Worrying about when and how it's going to happen is like placing an order at a restaurant and then chasing the waiter around while restating my order over and over. Of course, repeating it with increasing desperation isn't going to make the waiter bring my food any faster. It might even slow him down as he's constantly having to reassure me that he's got it.

Working on our dreams is the same way. We have to do our part by dreaming the dream, committing ourselves to achieving it, taking inspired action, and feeling the feelings of it already being our reality. It's difficult to be patient, but it can only help magnetize our dream to us quicker.

When I was single and ready to meet my soulmate, I felt more excited and impatient than I had felt in my life. I really wanted to meet my special someone to spend my life with. For years, I would wake up every day and wonder why he wasn't already here. As you can guess, this didn't help my situation. I was destined to meet my husband when the time was right and no amount of begging for him to get here was going to make the universe deliver him any sooner.

Instead, I had to realign my thoughts and feelings into the belief that the right man for me was already here. This was not an easy process. I wrote a list of all the wonderful qualities he possessed and the types of things we would enjoy doing together. I would talk to him while I was in the car as if he was there with me, and I would wish him sweet dreams each night before I went to sleep. At the same time, I started making myself unavailable to men who weren't a match for the energy I wanted in my most important relationship. It was definitely a learning curve, but now that I'm happily and passionately married to my soulmate, I can see that those decisions and that patience were worth it.

Derek and I are experiencing this lesson together now as we attempt to be patient on our journey of starting a family. Once we were married in 2017, we decided to start trying for a baby when we returned from our honeymoon. We figured that it would take 6–12 months to conceive naturally and decided to give it our best shot and see what unfolded. Instead of baby-conceiving bliss, we experienced increased disappointment and frustration as month after month went by without a baby on the way.

We met with doctors who tested us in every possible way for fertility and baby-making abilities. All the tests came back saying that we're very healthy and capable of conceiving naturally. So, we continued to try for another year without success. It may sound like fun, but keep in mind that this is a pretty stressful process. We're closely tracking my ovulation cycle, and I'm doing science experiments in the bathroom in the early morning, testing to see if I'm at peak ovulation. We even tried doing an intrauterine insemination (IUI) and it didn't work.

Feeling defeated, we had an exploratory conversation with an in-vitro fertilization (IVF) doctor. We endured more tests, learned a lot about human reproduction that we hadn't learned in school, and decided to go for it. At the time, this office was doing an IVF study that, if we met the criteria for the study, would enable us to have one round of IVF for free. We were very interested in that possibility and happily jumped through the hoops in hopes of making our dream come true. When we were on the last phase of testing, we awaited a critical phone call that would tell us for sure if we were accepted into the highly coveted study.

When the call came in, we were driving in traffic to a literacy night at a local elementary school in which we would both be leading presentations for the students and their families. Realizing it was the doctor's office, I put the phone on speaker mode so we could both participate. The nurse had called to tell us that my blood tests came back with great results, but that unfortunately we didn't qualify for the study. My heart immediately sank, and my head started to think of how to respond without bursting into tears. Before either of us could say anything, the nurse said, "The reason you don't qualify is because you're already pregnant."

Derek and I were shocked and overjoyed at this exciting news. She told us that they tested me for pregnancy just in case, and I was in fact pregnant! She even gave us the due date: June 6. We were so happy. We decided to only tell two people, my mom and my sister. Unable to contain our enthusiasm, we called them while we were in the car and shared the wonderful news. They were both very happy and excited for us. We felt like the luckiest people in the world and couldn't wait to meet our baby in the spring.

The first several weeks were great, although my body felt very tired and different. I was still able to do all of my regular workouts, appearances, and writing. I just needed to take more naps. Every day I felt so blessed to have a baby on the way. When it came time for our pregnancy check-up appointment, we were excited to see our baby's heartbeat for the first time. The day of the appointment, I had waves of pain in my lower abdomen. It was strong enough to make me sit down again right before we left to see the doctor. Determined to keep the appointment and learn our next steps, I pushed through the pain and went anyway.

When we arrived at the doctor's office, something didn't feel right to me. I had woken up with way more energy than I had for the past six weeks. That all changed in the afternoon when the extreme cramping began. I told the doctor what was happening, and after a few tests, she confirmed that we were in the process of losing the pregnancy. I was so surprised by the news that I couldn't fully process it. It was as if she was speaking another language and I could only understand a few words. Everything sounded like gibberish to me, but I could tell that it wasn't good news because of the look on her face and the soft tone of her voice. It felt like she was apologizing to me. After asking her questions about the same thing over and over in different ways, it finally started to set in: I was having a miscarriage.

The doctor left the room to give us a few minutes of privacy. I couldn't look at Derek. I could only look straight ahead at the wall. I could hear from his breathing that he was upset. If I turned to my left and saw his face, it would make the miscarriage real. I felt ashamed and scared to admit what was happening. Derek is the most amazing, thoughtful, loving person I've ever met, and I never want to disappoint him. He was so excited about becoming a dad. I felt like I had failed or had done something wrong that took that opportunity away from him. I felt silly for ever getting my hopes up about being parents. On top of all of that, I was in a great deal of pain but was told not to take anything for it because it could mask the symptoms of an ectopic pregnancy that would mean I'd have to be taken to the emergency room immediately to save my life.

It was a day that started with complete joy and excitement and ended with the worst possible news: we were losing our baby. I wasn't prepared for the physical and emotional pain that came with that experience. It seems like there are many resources online that will tell you about the emotional side of a miscarriage, and that's important. But over the five days that followed that appointment, the physical pain was almost unbearable. I kept praying that I could get through the physical pain so that I could then attend to the emotional pain.

To top it all off, we were contractually obligated to appear at a three-day event that weekend. I could've stayed home, but we would've lost over $4,000, and I didn't want that to happen on top of this tragedy. The doctor had me come in early every morning before the event for bloodwork to make sure that my hormones were going down. If so, that meant that there was no danger of an ectopic pregnancy and I could avoid emergency surgery. We were very lucky that we didn't have to go to the hospital, everything happened naturally over the course of five days.

So, there we were at a three-day event, trying to keep it together to be present for our Fans, sign books, and make kids smile while we were going through the most difficult experience we'd ever had. It felt like we were in an emotionally twisted horror movie. At first, we only told my mom and my sister. I couldn't talk about it without breaking down, and I needed to look put together for our event. Now I understood why people didn't share their pregnancy news until after three to four months—so they could avoid having to un-tell them if something went wrong.

It's been several months since that fateful day, and I can honestly say that it was the worst day of my life. Derek and I are so blessed that we have each other and that we were able to do our meet and greets and sign books that weekend so that our loss didn't negatively impact our business. Of course, I was sitting down most of the weekend, and Derek was taking good care of me throughout, as always. Later the following week, we were able to tell our other family members. They were incredibly supportive and encouraging. Eventually, I was able to open up about the experience with a few friends who shared with me that they had been through it as well. I was amazed at the number of women who have. It's such a difficult thing, and yet it seems like half of the women I know have lived through it.

For the first month, the sight of a pregnant woman triggered the feeling of the loss and made me feel sad. I've been compassionate with myself about my healing process. Being around kids and families never seemed to upset me, maybe because I'm so used to it being a children's author. I had some minor physical complications over the last few months, and I'm happy to say that I've recovered now. Derek and I are still hopeful and anticipating our next pregnancy. I'm a little scared, but I know that we will be okay no matter what. It doesn't make waiting any easier.

Every day I think about how wonderful I'll feel when we find out that we're pregnant again and how much love we're going to give that baby. I imagine what Derek's face will look like when we hear that great news and how strong and loving he will be as a father to our children one day. I look forward to that magical moment and remind myself to trust divine timing and to enjoy the present as well. It's a good practice in patience, and I know that it'll be worth it to start our family when the time is right.

Income and Influence

In many ways, the more income we attract, the more influence we can have. Money gives us more options, and we can all benefit from freedom of choice. By stabilizing our financial serenity, we free our energy to focus on having a greater impact in the world.

Always Carry Cash

I never used to have cash in my wallet. I was less intentional about being prepared and assumed that the world was moving in the direction of plastic, so I would, too. I also rarely had actual money and would rely on credit cards for everything while I was out. Of course, this irresponsible pattern eventually came back to bite me when my credit card bills grew and multiplied over time.

I don't remember what book I read it in, but somewhere I read about the wealth consciousness that comes with carrying a $100 bill in your wallet that you never spend. At first, I thought it was almost crazy to carry around that kind of cash (I was just out of grad school and didn't have a lot of money, after all). Then I started thinking about how it would feel to know that I always had some money in my pocket. I decided to give it a try.

At the time, I didn't have a $100 bill, so I decided that I would keep the first one that showed up in my world. It happened to be with the sale of my first book, *The Dreams Come True Journal*. A friend purchased four books and paid with a $100 bill. I delightedly tucked it into my wallet and was determined not to spend it no matter what. Having that money in my wallet gave me a level of confidence and security that I never experienced before. I knew that I would be alright no matter what.

A few years later, I attended a personal development conference that was focused on prosperity. One of the requirements was to bring in a $100 bill. I smiled knowing I would use the one in my wallet that I always had with me. On the day when the speaker called forth our $100 bills, it was fascinating to me how many people didn't bring one, brought the wrong bills, or asked to borrow one. I sat there with my $100 bill and was appalled when he had assistants light candles at the front of the room. He said that part of attracting money is being willing to let it go. He commanded that people stand up from their seats, line up, and proceed to the front of the room to burn their bills.

I was outraged. Here was a room of hundreds of people lining up to burn money, some of whom weren't even burning their own money! I stayed in my seat and made people climb over me to get into line. There was no way I was going to burn that special $100 bill that was the first money I had ever made as an author. No way. I thought about how much money was about to go up in flames and it made me feel ill. I estimated that there were 600 people at the event, and if each one was burning $100, that would be $60,000 completely wasted.

The people around me kept encouraging me to get in line with them and were implying that I would get in trouble if I disobeyed the sometimes-hot-headed speaker. I didn't care. I wasn't budging, and I couldn't believe that they were actually going to do it. I didn't care if he yelled at me in front of everyone or threw me out of the conference. I would rather walk out in front of the hotel and hand my $100 to a homeless person than burn it in that ballroom.

When the person at the front of the line approached the first candle and was about to burn his money, the speaker told everyone to stop and to blow out the candles. I was relieved when he told them to return to their seats. He said that this was a test and that they had all failed. He asked me why I hadn't followed his directions. I told him that I worked hard to earn that $100 bill and there was no way I was going to waste it like that. I'd rather gift it to someone who needed it than go along with the crowd and burn it.

He said that I'd done well and explained that if you're willing to burn money, you're not going to be able to hang on to money when you make it. He also shared that if people borrowed the money, that's what they do in life—come unprepared and ask someone else to cover them. If people didn't bring the right bills, they sabotage themselves by not following directions and that inhibits their ability to do their best with money. And for people who loaned out the $100 bills, they are sometimes too generous loaning their hard-earned money to people who don't want to work as hard as they do and often don't get it back. It was a game-changing moment for me. I realized that I no longer felt that I needed to please authority figures and that I wasn't afraid to stand out in the crowd.

A few years later, I was fulfilling my mom's dream of seeing Neil Diamond perform live in concert and had a little less cash than I normally did in my wallet ($115). Parking at the Hollywood Bowl that night was $20, something I didn't realize until we were already in the middle of the long line to park. I dug through my wallet and found that I was short (I never counted the $100 bill as part of my spending money). It was cash-only, and I didn't want my mom to pay for anything during her special night out, so I had to break my $100 bill to pay for the parking. I felt really sad to spend it after all those years of it keeping me company, especially since it was the first $100 bill I had earned as an author. I told myself I would make another $100 and replace it as soon as I could, and I'm happy to share that I did just that a few days later.

From that day forward, I resolved to always carry plenty of cash. As I'm debt-free, I prefer to pay with cash or a debit card. There are some instances (certain parking lots, taxis in Las Vegas, tipping valets and bellhops, etc.) where cash is still king. I never want to shortchange someone who helps me because I don't have enough cash to give them a well-deserved tip. Sometimes paying with cash will also net you a discount, and I'm a big fan of saving money. So, my advice to you is to always carry cash so you can be generous, feel prosperous, and get yourself out of a bind if you ever need to.

Give a Little, Make a Big Difference

When I was a kid, my mom was blessed to work for a wonderful man for many years. Mr. Stoides was a tall, dark-haired man from Greece with a deep accented voice, a kind face, and who smelled of expensive cologne. He was the most exotic person I'd ever met. He especially stood out in my small town of mostly native Virginians.

Mr. Stoides was an incredibly generous man. He would go on business trips around the world and would occasionally bring back small gifts for me and my sister. There were figurines from Japan, Swatch watches from London, and tiny dolls from Holland. I remember them well, particularly because these were considered treasures and my mom displayed them in her china cabinet where we couldn't ruin them by playing with them. That's where they still remain to this day.

Once, I was sick and had been to the doctor during a school day. My mom took my sister and me to the pharmacy to fill my prescription. I must've been around seven or eight years old at the time. We happened to run into Mr. Stoides. I wasn't feeling well, but he knew how to make me smile.

He pointed to a candy bar on display near the cash register and asked me if I liked that candy. I honestly didn't know because my family rarely bought candy (my mom focused on getting groceries with the limited income we had back then). So he picked one up for me and one up for my sister. Then, he pointed to another candy bar and asked if I liked that one. I said "yes," and he grabbed two of those. He asked the cashier to give him two bags. The cashier came back with two brown paper lunch bags, and Mr. Stoides handed one to each of us and said to fill them up with whatever candy bars we would like.

Julie and I couldn't believe it. We'd never been allowed to buy candy, much less to pick a bunch of candy bars to take home with us to enjoy. He laughed and smiled the whole time. He probably bought us ten candy bars each, which felt like a lifetime supply to us. We had never experienced that level of generosity before. Even though it probably didn't cost him much, it made a world of difference to me and my sister. We still laugh remembering that day.

I kept in touch with Mr. Stoides throughout my high school, undergrad, and grad school years. I was inspired by the way he took care of his family, deeply cared about his employees and their families, and was a successful businessman. Sadly, he passed away several years ago. I will always remember how he talked to me with such kindness and wisdom in his accent and made a sad and scary day a happy memory.

His story is a great reminder that you don't have to give a lot in order to make a big impact. It's often the little things we do that can make the biggest difference in the lives of others. Just making someone smile is a worthy pursuit. And if you can make their heart smile, even better!

Safety and Serenity

There is a monumental amount of peace that comes from knowing that your finances are in order. The financial serenity we feel when we're actively managing our finances carries over into every area of our lives, attracting more prosperity so we can create a legacy and make an even bigger difference.

Financial Peace

Choosing not to have a spending plan and live within your means is a sophisticated form of self-sabotage. One of the best decisions my husband and I made when we got married was to become debt-free. This powerful choice set us on a path to financial serenity and eventual wealth.

We didn't want to owe anything to anyone. We wanted the freedom to save, give, spend, and invest all of our income without paying for things done in the past, with interest. We wanted the security of having a Serenity Fund (otherwise known as an Emergency Fund) to weather life's storms without financial stress. We wanted the comfort of knowing that we were escrowing for upcoming expenses, and when the time comes to buy a vehicle, bring a baby home from the hospital, or pay our insurance, we have the money ready and waiting (and accruing interest!) in savings.

I used to think I was being smart and sophisticated by using credit cards and getting points or miles for my purchases. I rationalized it by saying I'd be spending the money anyway, so why not get some of it back? But I was kidding myself because eventually there would be a month that I couldn't afford to pay the balance in full. And the next month wasn't any easier. Before I knew it, I had fallen back into debt again. Having debt makes you a prisoner by shackling your income to paying an ever-growing bill, limiting your options. It also makes paying bills and accounting more complicated. It was all a sticky mess, and I'm grateful that we worked our way out of it.

Truth be told, I've worked my way out of debt with focused intention three times in my life. And each time I got into debt, I felt like I had a "good reason." But those excuses, no matter how valid I believed they were, didn't pay the bills or make me feel any better as the balances added up.

I got my first credit card in college. On campus, there seemed to be credit card salespeople set up regularly everywhere—the quad, the university center, the bookstore. They were almost inescapable. I ignored them for a while, but then I got curious about the sign-up gifts on the table.

I came from a family of humble means and wanted to get a shirt with my college's name on it, but I couldn't afford it with the expense of books, tuition, and food. "Just sign up for a credit card for 'emergencies' and the shirt can be yours right now." I actually thought I was being responsible! My delusional self was happy to get the T-shirt (which didn't even fit properly) and vowed not to use the "emergency" card when it arrived in the mail.

But then life happened, and it was all too easy to use the plastic. I wanted to get some new clothes and didn't have enough to cover the purchase. The clothes were on a great sale, so I rationalized going into debt as a smart choice to take advantage of the savings. I was a responsible 18-year-old who was trying to be smart with money. But I also wanted to look cool and didn't have the money to pay for items at the time, so I continued rationalizing and using the credit card. Then, with additional sign-up gifts tempting me, the credit cards began to multiply in my wallet.

When I finally realized what interest was, I had $2,000 in debt and was making the minimum payments every month, not even making a dent in the balance. So, I decided not to use the card and to pay if off as quickly as I could. It took me two years to pay it off on my meager salary, and I went into my senior year of college debt-free (except for student loans). I assured myself that I wouldn't go down the dark path of debt again.

A few years later, I had graduated with my master's degree and was working in Washington, D.C., when I had the opportunity to move to California. It had been one of my childhood dreams to live in Southern California and it was one of my biggest goals. If I passed up the opportunity, I didn't know when I would get it again. I didn't know anyone there, but I felt in my heart and soul that I belonged there and would flourish. I didn't have enough savings to cover the expense of moving myself, my car, my cats, and my stuff across the country. So, I pulled the credit card out of the drawer and declared this opportunity an emergency.

Moving to California was one of the best choices I ever made, but it would've been an easier transition if I had been saving up for it more aggressively. It took me another nine years to become debt-free, including credit cards, my car, and my student loans. I was elated when I made the last student loan payment. Let me tell you, driving a fully paid-off car felt so much better than having payments. I was finally able to start saving and investing all the money that I had previously been putting toward debt payments.

Then, I decided I wanted to consider buying a house. I was young and dumb and believed that it was smarter than renting. I had no idea that the true cost of homeownership is almost double your monthly mortgage payment. I had intuitive feelings that I shouldn't jump in yet, but I ignored them in the excitement of having my own home. It was quite a shock to my system going from being completely debt-free to having an enormous mortgage and a drained savings account that mostly went toward the down payment. I was making good money in the corporate world, but I still didn't seem to have enough to keep up with the lavish spending of my colleagues at the time.

When I started to awaken to the fact that my life, and wanting to be an entrepreneur, wasn't working with all of this added debt and pressure, my American dream of homeownership became more like a nightmare. It was compounded by happening in 2008 when the real estate market tanked only a few months after I had moved in. I continued to use credit cards for household expenses while paying off the balances every month.

Several years later when I got divorced and moved, I relied on credit cards to pay bills and tried to pamper myself a little during a difficult time in my life. I continued paying them off every month until I couldn't anymore, and then the balances really ran up. I was an entrepreneur learning about business, attending conferences, investing in creating new books, and spending a lot on marketing costs with each new launch. My expenses for the most part seemed like smart investments in my future, but I couldn't afford them and felt ashamed when the credit card bills came in every month.

Once, I was checking into a nice hotel to attend a conference out of state. I had just gotten to my room when a piece of paper was slid under my door saying that my credit card company declined the hold due to insufficient funds. I had checked my balances before leaving for my flight and knew I had enough to cover the trip. I called the credit card company and was informed that I had gotten close to hitting my credit limit on a different card with a much smaller balance. It had triggered my other credit cards to automatically decrease my credit limits. I couldn't believe it! I paid more than the minimum balances every month and had never been late with a payment. Unfortunately, none of that mattered. There was nothing I could do to change it.

I felt embarrassed and hopeless. Because of the way I watched my family struggle financially when I was growing up, not having enough money is a big trigger for me. I was freaking out and called my mom to brainstorm what to do. I remembered that I had been investing heavily into my retirement fund while I was in the corporate world and we agreed that although it wasn't ideal, this was my best option. I called my financial planner and told him what happened and my proposed solution. I felt ashamed and even cried, but I had to find the money quickly so I could make things right with the hotel.

After I confirmed that the paperwork to take an early withdrawal from my retirement fund was being faxed over, I went to the front desk and asked to speak with the hotel manager. I showed him the letter, apologized for the inconvenience, and told him that the money would be in my account in twenty-four hours. He was very kind and told me that it would be fine. I was relieved to have it resolved but stressed about what to do when I got home to actually fix the problem.

Other conference attendees spent their first night at the hotel mingling, having dinner, or relaxing by the pool. I spent mine in a panic trying to clean up a mess I had created, while being honest about the reality of my situation. It was terrible having to tell the truth about my mistakes to my mom, my financial planner, and the hotel manager. I decided that I would never put myself in that precarious position again.

When I returned from the conference, I was on fire. I went through my belongings in storage and sold as much as I could bear to part with. I started doing some project work on the side to supplement my income. I cut out every non-essential expense to pay off the debt forever.

By the time I got married to my soulmate a few years later, I had paid off over sixty percent of my debt. I had been working so hard for so long. I was embarrassed to share the financial mistakes of my past, but my husband was wonderful about it. We started reading and listening to Dave Ramsey and used his "Debt Snowball" method of getting out of debt. We paid it off together with focused intensity and then built our Serenity Fund while building our business completely debt-free.

It made a huge difference combining our finances and creating monthly spending plans. Once we planned our expenditures for the month, we could see the areas where we were spending on things that weren't bringing us peace or joy and didn't feel worth it compared to our exciting goals. So, we went through our home and sold everything we didn't use or love. I went back through the items I had kept in storage and was able to sell seventy-five percent of it. We cut our costs by getting on a family phone plan, cancelling cable, and being more conscious of our spending. We took Dave Ramsey's Financial Peace University classes and stopped loaning money to people who we originally thought we were helping, but were really just enabling their self-destructive behaviors and poor decision-making. It built our confidence and communication as a couple and put us on the right track for our future.

Now we save up for everything we do personally and professionally. If we don't have the money for it, we don't do it. And I finally cut up and closed my credit cards for good. Every time I became debt-free in the past, I worked so hard to do it and still kept the cards open "just in case." I've finally learned that it's my responsibility to save up "just in case" and that the financial peace we feel from only buying what we can afford, only keeping what we use and love, and saving for our future is better than anything I ever put on a credit card.

We look forward to updating our net worth each month and strategizing our spending plan on EveryDollar (the app that Dave Ramsey's organization created to make budgeting and tracking spending easy). We do it for our personal and professional life and it provides such a feeling of clarity, union, and purpose. It gets easier every time we do it. It's reassuring to be on the same page and moving forward with a shared vision for our future.

Make a Massive Positive Difference

Knowing that you have enough and can help others is one of the best feelings you can achieve with money. The warm and cuddly feelings of safety and serenity buoy you up at times when your world may feel like it's turning upside down. Money is not the most important thing, but having more money can help you make a bigger difference in the world. For example, you can do a lot more good with $1 million than you can with $10, yet so many of us don't want to look like we're doing things for the money. I find this to be especially true with authors. They'll say that they're not worried about the money and that they're only writing their book to help kids.

What if you can help kids AND make a lot of money, which would enable you to write more books and to help MORE kids? That's the reality that we deny ourselves when we cling to the statement that we don't care about money because we don't want to look greedy. It's not greedy to want to create a better life for your family while making a positive difference in the world. I think it's very noble to serve humanity in that way, and you deserve to make a profit from your art and your efforts. The bigger profit you make, the bigger difference you can also make. There's nothing wrong with that!

Prosperity in Action

1. Put a $100 bill in your wallet and don't spend it. It's there to remind you of the abundance in your life.
2. Create a spending plan using Dave Ramsey's EveryDollar app (It's free!). Honor your abundance to attract more.
3. Organize your cash in your wallet. Keep your wallet neat and clean (Good-bye, random receipts!). I like to keep my presidents all facing the same direction and in order according to dollar value—one-dollar bills in the front and $100 bills in the back. This also ensures that I don't accidentally grab the wrong bill and overpay for something.
4. Start tracking your net worth each month. If you don't measure something, it's hard to change it for the better.
5. Build a Serenity Fund to cover unforeseen expenses. Figure out how much it would take for you to live for six months and set it aside so that you always have money on hand for emergencies.

Prosperity on Social Media

LinkedIn is my favorite social media platform to encourage Prosperity. Years ago, I used LinkedIn as a self-updating address book to maintain contacts with former colleagues when I'd move on to new companies. In recent years, LinkedIn has become a much more popular platform that professionals use to stay on top of their industries and to promote their businesses. I've received multiple business opportunities as a result of my presence on LinkedIn and find it to be the platform that contributes most to my prosperity.

Let's Connect on LinkedIn

https://www.Linkedin.com/in/SheriFink/

PANACHE

Never let anyone dim your sparkle.

I've always loved the word, "panache." Not only the way it sounds so fancy, but also because of its meaning of "flamboyant confidence of style or manner." What would it be like if you left your house every day feeling like a million bucks? What different choices would you make in your day if you felt gorgeous, confident, fit, and passionate everywhere you went? When we add more panache to our lives, we feel more vibrant and alive. That confidence can't help but spill out onto the world around us and attract new people, exciting opportunities, and great hair days. Who doesn't want that?

Meaning and Magnetism

Everything that's worth doing in life can be done with style and joy if we connect with the reasons for why we do what we do and make them matter.

Magical, Meaningful, and Memorable

One of my goals for anything I do personally or professionally is to make it magical, meaningful, and memorable. Magical means that it feels like an extraordinary experience, something beyond the every day. Meaningful means that it will be more than a superficial experience, something that touches me and others on an emotional level. And memorable means that it's something worth remembering.

I first came up with the phrase, "magical, meaningful, and memorable," when we were planning our wedding and I was describing how I wanted it to feel. I've used it ever since to set the intentions for our author appearances, book signings, speaking engagements, family vacations, date nights, and even outings with friends.

I find it's valuable to set intentions before planning major events and activities and to check in with myself to see if the things I'm doing meet the criteria. Because if they don't, why do them at all? We have such limited time on this planet. I'd rather spend it doing something special, touching the hearts of others, and making happy memories as opposed to just going through the motions.

Keep the Faith

Sometimes it feels like things can take forever. You have an idea and feel as if it's already real, but reality hasn't caught up yet. I'm taking action and making progress every day, though. Even when the steps are small, they're still steps in the right direction. Eventually I'll get to where I'm meant to go.

It just seems like many things in our modern world should be easier than they are and should be faster than they are. Goals take the time they take. Time is going to pass whether we're making progress or not, so we might as well be patient and continue taking action toward our dreams. Practice having complete faith. One day we'll look up and be amazed at what we've accomplished.

Roses in the Airport

I've traveled a lot throughout my career and one of my favorite things to see while I'm away is the reunions of people being picked up from the airport. In particular, I love it when I come through the gate to baggage claim and see people eagerly awaiting their loved one's arrival. For years, I watched as people waited with flowers and balloons and had their slow-motion run to greet their loved one. I called it "Roses in the Airport," and I hoped that one day I would be with a man who had enough confidence, consideration, and charisma to wait for me in the airport to welcome me home.

Shortly after Derek and I started dating, I was scheduled to be away on travel for three weeks. I was excited about our newly forming relationship as well as my upcoming adventures. When I left for the trip, I hoped that time would make the heart grow fonder and that he would miss me as much as I knew I was going to miss him. It was a fabulous trip that included an awards ceremony, an experience with a baby tiger at a wildlife preserve, and fun times with my family celebrating Thanksgiving.

We talked a few times briefly while I was away, but my schedule and the time zone difference made it complicated to connect for any substantive conversation. I couldn't wait to see him again. When my plane landed back at LAX, and I walked through the baggage claim doors, I was pleasantly surprised to find my new boyfriend standing there with a bouquet of flowers and a bright neon green sign on which he had written in bold: *"Award-winning Author and Baby Tiger Handler – Sheri Fink!"* Seeing him there waiting for me so sweetly, and without worry about what other people would think, melted my heart. I cried when I saw him there (just like I'm doing right now). We've been inseparable ever since.

Weird and Wonderful

There's nothing wrong with being different or "weird." When we let go of concern or worry about what others think about us, we free ourselves to be the weird and wonderful people we were born to be.

Being Weird

Confession: I am weird and always have been (in case you haven't already figured it out). I took a business quiz online the other day to see what type of leader I am and found it hilarious when the result came back in big, bold letters: "You are Weird." I already knew that, and it made me laugh. But I didn't always feel secure in my weirdness. Actually, it wasn't until the last several years that I started truly embracing my uniqueness and not hiding it.

As a kid, I simultaneously wanted to blend in to be accepted and stand out to be the person I knew I was on the inside. I felt very confused about this tug-of-war going on in my feelings. When I discovered Weird Al Yankovic, I felt like I had found a kindred spirit. Here was someone who was bringing joy to people all over the world by being his unique, "weird" self. I was fascinated with his music videos and clever wordplay, transforming popular songs into hilarious parodies. I still smile when I see him show up in pop culture and hear his songs. I loved his self-confidence. He didn't seem to care how silly he might look. He just went for it.

The first time I saw him in concert, I didn't dare post about it on social media. I didn't think that my friends would think it was "cool." Recently, Derek took me to see him perform at the Hollywood Bowl, and I proudly posted about how much I like Weird Al and how much fun we were having. In the comments, I discovered tons of friends who also liked him. I was surprised to see so many people from high school commenting. If only I had been more honest about what I authentically liked way back then, I might've had high school friends to connect with about his music and might've embraced my own weirdness sooner. As Weird Al's popular song says, it's okay (and even advisable) to "dare to be stupid."

Goodbye, "Good Girl"

Insecurity robs you of your sense of self, your authenticity, and your hope. You make different choices about the world and your place in it when you feel inferior and unworthy. Having a lack of confidence not only makes you waste your precious energy constantly questioning yourself, but also diminishes your luck. When your mind is busy criticizing you, it doesn't have the awareness to scan your environment for opportunities. And luck only finds you when you're ready and receptive.

Feeling insecure closes you off from making real connections because you censor your self-expression, worrying about how you think the listener is going to perceive you. It's exhausting to hold back who you really are and try to please everyone all the time. Not being your authentic self and saying how you truly feel, think, and desire can get you stuck in bad relationships, jobs, friendships, and situations that make you feel sad, hopeless, and depressed. It's a stressful way to live. And beyond the negative impact on you, it's bad for the rest of us because we never really get the opportunity to know the real you.

I know exactly how it feels because I spent the first 30+ years of my life trapped in my mind, worrying what everyone would think, and feeling afraid that I was too much, not enough, and unworthy at the same time. I think one of the things I feared was really standing in my power. It felt like such a big responsibility to own my life. I didn't want to turn into one of those people who seemed bratty or entitled. So, I would humbly accept whatever I was given and tried not to become a burden to anyone. If I didn't know what I wanted or what I even liked, then who was I to say "no, thanks" to anyone or anything? I believe it started in childhood with the intention to be a "good girl," but being self-confident and authentic doesn't make you a "bad girl." It makes you smart, happy, and successful.

I've found that authenticity is the key to happiness in life. I feel like my life went from black and white to technicolor when I decided to release my authentic, rainbow, unicorn-loving, pink, and sparkly self from the prison she had been in since childhood. It was like arriving in Oz and embracing who I really was for the first time.

I think I was holding back in order to be accepted. I worked in corporate offices and saw how people who were "different" weren't promoted or included in the important decisions. I didn't want to be left out due to my hair color. As a woman working in historically male-dominated industries, I wanted to be respected by my clients and colleagues. I didn't want to call, what I perceived to be, unnecessary and potentially negative attention to myself in the workplace. I conformed to survive and then to thrive in those environments.

Magical things started to happen in my writing career when I realized how limited I felt in the corporate world and how much freedom I would have as an entrepreneur. When I focused on being authentic instead of being accepted, I started to feel better about myself. I felt confident and able to empower others to embrace their authentic selves. This decision truly changed my life.

I love the quote by Dr. Seuss that says, "Be who you are and say how you feel because those who mind don't matter and those who matter don't mind." Of course, there will be misguided people who just don't like you. But those narrow-minded people wouldn't have liked you no matter what you did. So, don't worry about them. The important thing is that *you* like you and that you share your true self with the world.

Don't Worry about the Muggles

I'm often asked by aspiring authors and other big dreamers how to handle naysayers. Every one of us has a story (at least one) about someone not believing in us and laughing in our faces when we told them the big, exciting stuff we were in the process of manifesting into our lives. The thing is, no one's opinion matters except yours.

If you have a big dream in your heart, it's probably there for a reason and there must be a way to make it come true, even if your circumstances look bleak at the moment. The best thing to do is to treat other people's opinions as none of your business and go about the business of making things happen. Get so focused on working on your dream that you don't even hear them anymore. Remember, dogs only bark at cars as they pass by.

Don't worry about the muggles. Not everyone is as magical as you. Just like in the Harry Potter series, the muggles are the ordinary humans. It's not their fault, and there's nothing you can do to make them see your magic. Just do the work to live your dream and lead by example. Once you've accomplished your big goal, they may ask you how you did it, and then you can share some of your magic. Until then, stay focused and don't let anyone or anything drain your precious energy. Let go of the anchor of needing other people's approval. It will only hold you back, weaken your resolve, and make you resentful toward them. You need all of your emotional and physical energy to propel you forward to your dream.

It also helps to surround yourself with other magical people who believe in you. I nicknamed my sister Julie "Little Big Sister" because she's a fierce supporter of me. She and my mom are incredibly inspiring women who are also two of my very best friends. I know that I can call them anytime and say anything. They will always be there for me and will always try to do what's in my best interest. It's wonderful knowing I have friends and family who have my back on the same level that I have theirs.

Style and Substance

When we find ways to bring more fun, joy, and playfulness into our daily lives, we sparkle with our own unique style and empower others to shine their special light as well.

You're Never Fully Dressed without a Smile

When I was in kindergarten, I was obsessed with the movie *Annie*. I sang the songs and wanted to wear the clothes that Annie wore in the movie. At the time, many of my clothes were hand-me-downs from my cousins (I even had boy clothes!). When I was younger, my mom made some of my outfits, but once she started working full-time again, she didn't have as much time. One day my mom surprised me with my very own Annie dress that she had made for me. I was over the moon! I wore that dress as often as possible (at least once a week). It's funny because I was so quiet, self-conscious, and shy, but I loved wearing that dress so much that I didn't consider or care what anyone else thought about it.

I felt so special wearing the Annie dress, partly because my mom took the time to make it for me, but also because I loved Annie and wanted to have her charm, confidence, and charisma. When I wore that red dress, I felt like a little bit of her spunkiness was granted to me. And no amount of judgment from anyone else could change that for me. I was relentless about wearing that dress until I grew out of it and had to gift it to my little sister.

I guess I was a cosplayer before I even knew what that was. I still love dressing up in "fancy" clothes and wearing costumes. Luckily, I have a career that enables me to combine a bunch of my passions. That dress was so unique, and I felt incredibly joyful even thinking about wearing it. I'm not sure I have anything in my wardrobe today that's as exciting as that dress was for me as a child, but it's an important lesson. What if we all could wear clothes that made us feel unstoppable? What if we all could take such extraordinary care of loving ourselves to the extent that other people's opinions about us wouldn't matter? That's the way I want to feel every day.

A friend brought the *Annie* soundtrack in for show-and-tell at school one day, and all I could talk about at home was how much I wanted that record. I remember when my parents surprised me with it, and I immediately ripped the protective plastic off the cardboard album cover. My dad reacted with a "nooooooo." I was confused because I knew (from looking at my friend's album) that the cardboard opened up to display scenes from the movie, and I loved looking at the pictures. That was also a valuable lesson for me at five years old. Sometimes people will tell you not to do something, and they have honorable intentions, but they don't have all of the information to make the decision for you.

I'm happy to share that I had the pleasure of meeting Aileen Quinn, the actress who played Annie, a few years ago. Her band was performing at an event I was signing at. (What luck!) I was very excited and nervous to meet her. I actually started crying when I talked with her. She was sweet and welcoming and didn't seem to mind my rainbow hair at all. She closed her performance with a rendition of "Tomorrow" from the movie and made my childhood dream come true.

Breaking the Rules

When I was little girl, I was so proud to be a Brownie in the Girl Scouts. I remember we drove someplace that felt far away to have a special Girl Scout celebration day with girls from other troops traveling from the surrounding area. We painstakingly made crafts the week before that we were told we would exchange with other girls at the event.

Being shy and self-conscious at the time, I was nervous about how this interaction would go. And I wasn't too happy to give away the beautiful art project that I had just made. But I decided that I would do my best. On the day of the event, I was excited. The theme was "Up, Up, and Away" and the patch had hot air balloons on it. Imagine my disappointment when we arrived and I quickly discovered that I was not going to get to see a hot air balloon in person for the first time. I guess they just used those images for the marketing of the event. I learned something valuable about marketing to kids: underpromise and overdeliver.

When we arrived at the event, there were troops of girls all over. We exited the bus and followed our troop leader to the designated location for our troop. On the way there, I ran into a friend from my neighborhood who was in a different troop. She asked if I wanted to trade crafts, and I eagerly agreed. She gave me a cute pencil with mini pom-poms glued on it to look like a colorful caterpillar with tiny googly eyes. I felt proud of myself that I had achieved the goal of exchanging crafts with a girl from another troop, and so early in the day before anyone else. I felt that I could relax and enjoy the day now that I did what I was supposed to do.

The troop leader saw me smiling at my new possession and promptly burst my bubble. She asked me what I was holding. I proudly showed it to her and told her it was made by my friend, and I pointed over to her. She became angry and said that I was supposed to wait to trade with a girl in a specific troop that she had chosen. I tried to explain that I simply did what was asked of me, and that my friend was so happy with my gift that it made me feel happy, too. But she was upset and determined to make an example out of me. She told the rest of my troop not to break the rules like I did. Of course, no one had bothered to explain the rules to us. If they had, I would've been on top of it because that's the kind of kid I was.

I felt embarrassed and confused by her disappointment in me. I felt proud of myself for being bold and accomplishing the goal without any adult needing to strike up the conversation or set up the situation for me. Looking back on it, I feel like the troop leader could've applauded my entrepreneurial spirit and, knowing that I was a very shy child, reinforced my courage. Instead, she inadvertently gave me an opportunity to question authority at a young age. I still have that googly eyed caterpillar pencil as a reminder to go my own way and do what feels right for me. I can't remember the troop leader's name or face. Her misguided words still sting so many years later, but the clear memory of my friend's smile was worth it.

Fun and Fearlessness

Fear attempts to keep us "safe," playing small when we are meant for great things. Life is more fun and fulfilling when we have adventures ahead of us, give ourselves permission to enjoy the ride, and celebrate our successes along the way.

Let's Have an Adventure

I'm the kind of person who needs some fun and adventure in my life. Daily life can sometimes feel monotonous unless you have something special to look forward to in the near future. I love the anticipation of a unique experience coming up and relish the memories I have of doing fun things with my family and friends. It's good to break out of your comfort zone and do things that make you feel more alive and present, as you often feel when doing completely new things. I have an Adventure List, and every year I seek to check off a few experiences that really get my heart pumping.

Here are a few of the dream adventures and activities I have achieved so far that may inspire you to create your own Adventure List:

1. Taking hip-hop dance lessons
2. Flying in a hot air balloon over vineyards in Temecula
3. Scuba diving in Kauai
4. Doing the Sydney Bridge Climb in Australia
5. Taking a cruise on the Disney Dream
6. Indoor skydiving at Universal City
7. Holding a baby tiger at a wildlife sanctuary in Miami
8. Playing with a penguin at an aquarium in Arizona
9. Holding a koala in Cairns
10. Feeding a kangaroo in Sydney
11. Riding a camel in the desert
12. Zip lining Superman-style on a two-mile-long zip line in Puerto Rico

13. Having dinner inside the Eiffel Tower in Las Vegas and in Paris, France
14. Catching a foul ball at a Major League Baseball game
15. Taking guitar lessons
16. Having couple's paint-night lessons
17. Flying in a helicopter on the Big Island
18. Seeing active volcanos erupting in Hawaii
19. Touring the legendary Louvre Museum in Paris
20. Dining in Club 33 with my family at Disneyland
21. Jet skiing in Miami
22. Snorkeling at the Great Barrier Reef in Cairns
23. Eating Baked Alaska in New Orleans
24. Feeding a giraffe at a zoo in Palm Desert
25. Touring Memphis and Graceland with my mom
26. Seeing Harry Potter and the Cursed Child on Broadway in NYC
27. Experiencing Disneyland Paris in France
28. Going old-school roller skating while wearing a tutu
29. Holding a seahorse in Hawaii
30. Planting a pineapple in Maui

These are examples of things that I put on my Adventure List and then sought out to experience. One of the things I love to do is add a day to any business trip at a new destination so that we can have a day dedicated to adventure. It's something to look forward to as we're achieving our business goals and gives us a much better feel for the place we're visiting. What kinds of fun experiences do you want to have? Where do you want to travel? What do you want to eat? Where do you want to celebrate? In what small ways could you incorporate fun and adventure into your weekly or monthly goals?

It's always nice to have something to look forward to. Think about the way you feel as you're counting down the days to your next vacation. You can feel that excitement and anticipation more often when you plan smaller outings and excursions. It could be as simple as taking turns with your spouse planning romantic date nights or as elaborate as planning a once-in-a-lifetime cruise around the world. The goal is to choose activities that light you up and make you feel alive (maybe even a little nervous!). The more excited you feel about it, the better.

Do some research and keep the details handy for when you're ready to book your adventure. It doesn't have to be anything elaborate or expensive. You can tour a local museum you've always been curious about, visit the beach and watch the surfers catch some waves, have a picnic in a local park, try out the new ice cream place in town, attend a free workshop or lecture, take yourself for a nature walk, or simply visit your local zoo.

Sprinkle the fun throughout your calendar, maybe with a goal of doing at least one fun thing each month. It could be something you do alone, with a friend, with a spouse, with a sibling, or with your entire family. Make your activity reservations and then get busy focusing on other things. The fun day will arrive, and you will have so many accomplishments to celebrate.

When I have adventures, I love to take photos. I feel so much joy in doing the things that I've planned, and I want to relive those memories over and over. If photos are your thing, take lots of them throughout your experience. If you prefer to be completely present and not take any photos, that's great, too. Just savor every moment of your juicy experience and watch how relaxed and joyful you become as a result. Having fun is nourishing to our souls and is a great reminder that playfulness can be a part of our lives no matter our age.

And, don't be afraid to continue adding to your list as new ideas pop up. My list shrinks and then grows every year as I cross some adventures off and think of more. There's no rush to achieve this list. It's just a tool that's there for you to reference in order to add more fun to your life.

Enjoy the Ride

Several years ago, I had the privilege of taking my nephew to Disneyland for the first time. It's an annual tradition that my sister and I celebrate her birthday at Disneyland. She flies in from Virginia, and we have a blast. Since the day her son was born, we looked forward to the magical moment when he would be old enough to enjoy it with us. Our parameters were that he had to be able to walk all day without relying on a stroller, able to go to the bathroom on his own (no diapers), and old enough to remember it. When he turned seven, we decided that the time was right.

He had heard stories about the park and had seen commercials for years. He was also a big fan of Mickey Mouse thanks to the retro cartoons our mom's friend gifted him when he was little. As the day approached, he grew more and more excited. He couldn't wait to meet Mickey Mouse and go on amusement park rides for the first time. When we arrived at the park, and he saw the castle for the first time, we knew it was going to be a special day of dreams coming true, both for him and for us.

But things shifted a bit when we got in line for rides. This adorable little boy, who was so excited to be there, was afraid to ride the rides. Even the Fantasy Land rides were too scary and intimidating for him. My sister and I didn't know what to do. It looked like our day was going to be a power struggle between trying to convince him to give things a try and him being adamant that he wouldn't ride.

So, we decided to proceed with getting into lines and telling him that he could step through and wait for us while we rode if he wanted to. We would've had one of us wait with him if he chose not to ride, but wanted him to make the choice for himself. Our strategy worked. He would carefully consider his options while we focused on other conversations in the lines and then he would sit down with us and ride the rides. Even though he was visibly nervous, he always seemed to enjoy the ride after it was over.

Then we went to the biggest, scariest one of them all: Splash Mountain. It was a hot day and we really wanted to ride it. Plus, my sister only gets to visit Disneyland once a year and didn't want to miss out. We told him we'd be waiting in the line together and that he could step through the log and wait for us. All the way through the Fast Pass lane, he hemmed and hawed about how he didn't want to ride this one and it was too scary. We agreed that it was intimidating and that he didn't have to. We also told him about the fun stuff inside the mountain once you got beyond the hills.

When we stepped up to get on the ride, I instructed him to walk through the log and wait right there in the exit for us. To our great shock, he actually sat down in the ride! We were excited to see him act so bravely and knew that he would love it. As soon as we got to the start of the big hill (where the animatronic vultures are plotting your demise), he started crying and screaming, "Let me off of here!" at the top of his lungs. He had huge tears rolling down his cheeks, the biggest I've ever seen. He kept crying despite our reassurance that it was going to be okay and even fun.

One of the things I noticed in that moment and throughout the day is the way he rode the rides: with his arms tightly wrapped around anything they could reach and with his head down, bracing for cover. It was as if he was trying to shrink himself down and hold on so tightly to keep himself safe. He did it even on the kiddie rides, and it made me think about how much fun he could be having if he wasn't so afraid.

I had an epiphany as we were climbing the hill on Splash Mountain and hearing his wails for help: up until that point, I was living my life the way that he was riding the rides. I was holding on for dear life, trying to make myself smaller and less noticeable, and screaming and crying for help when things got hard, even though I could handle it. It was a bright light bulb moment for me. I decided that from that moment on, I would ride every ride, and even the ride of life, with my hands up in the air cheering and laughing.

I told him that everything was okay. "Look at me, I'm not even going to hold on!" And I threw my arms up in the air on a ride for the first time in my life. I wanted to model brave behavior for him. I wanted to feel bold. I was excited to be riding the ride, why shouldn't I fully embody that sensation?

As soon as we splashed down, the tears stopped (although he had a few still on his cheeks), and he started laughing. He had so much fun watching the animals sing and dance and hearing us scream as water splashed us. We all had a wonderful time and he taught me a valuable lesson in life.

We're all on this ride together, and we know that it has steep hills, dips, twists, and turns. We can choose to try to hide and close our eyes, or we can choose to sit up straight, put our hands in the air, and scream our heads off as we whoosh through the air. Are there areas in your life where you're playing small? Trying to keep yourself "safe?" Taking things way too seriously? Predicting doom and gloom when there's a possibility that everything will be okay? Holding on for dear life so tightly that you forget that you're supposed to be having fun? From now on, arms up on rides and in life!

Celebrate Your Successes

Working on a dream can be a long process. Depending on what you're accomplishing, it could be one year, four years, eight years, or twenty years before your dream officially comes true. If we wait to celebrate until the dream is fulfilled, we will be waiting a long time and may lose steam along the way. What works for me is to celebrate progress and milestones along the way.

These celebrations can be rewards for achieving a milestone, such as hitting the halfway mark on the wordcount for the book you're writing, completing and sending your applications for college, booking your first client, paying off your credit card, or moving into your new place. You don't have to wait until you've achieved the whole goal in order to acknowledge yourself for the positive changes you're making.

For example, I'm dedicating this week to writing this book and taking extraordinary care of myself. Neither of these things would happen if I didn't plan the time, say no to other opportunities and distractions, and encourage myself to keep writing no matter what. My focus is on workouts and wordcounts with the goal of writing 10,000 words. My reward for achieving that milestone is a visit to an animal sanctuary where my husband and I will get to meet several different types of monkeys, followed by a tour, barrel wine tasting, and picnic at a nearby winery. I'm so excited about the celebratory adventure that I've already written 18,778 words, and it's only Thursday! Setting up rewards for yourself honors your progress, gives you a dash of fun, and keeps you motivated to keep going until you achieve your dream.

Panache in Action

1. Create a vision board using images of things you want to be, do, and have in life. Let it reflect your personal style and have fun with it. (This can be a poster, a scrapbook, a digital collage, a Pinterest board, etc.)
2. Make a Dream/Adventure List – What do you want to be, do, and have in your lifetime?
3. Think of one area in your life where you can choose to throw your hands up and enjoy the ride. What action can you take (or stop taking) that will improve the quality of your experience?
4. List ways you would love to celebrate the achievement of your goals. Then visualize (see and feel) yourself living those celebrations in every juicy detail. Keep this list as a reference for your next success and have fun checking them off as you go along collecting magical, meaningful, and memorable experiences.

Panache on Social Media

Instagram is my favorite social media platform to encourage Panache. Instagram is heavily photo-driven and features more visual content than the other social media platforms. It's the best place to showcase your unique style and to connect with others who resonate with the things you most love. Instagram is easy to learn and is one of the most fun platforms to use.

Let's Connect on Instagram

https://www.Instagram.com/Sheri_Fink   @Sheri_Fink

https://www.Instagram.com/WhimsicalWorldBooks   @WhimsicalWorldBooks

Your Bliss Awaits

"This is my wish for you: Comfort on difficult days, smiles when sadness intrudes, rainbows to follow the clouds, laughter to kiss your lips, sunsets to warm your heart, hugs when spirits sag, beauty for your eyes to see, friendships to brighten your being, faith so that you can believe, confidence for when you doubt, courage to know yourself, patience to accept the truth, love to complete your life." ~ Ralph Waldo Emerson

Life is truly amazing, and we can embrace our limitless possibilities when we are authentic, take inspired action, and create magic for ourselves and others. No matter how much we think we'd prefer it (and how much social media shows us otherwise), life isn't meant to be a series of perfect, bliss-filled days. There will always be some rain mixed in with the sunshine. It's meant to be all of it—the good days, the bad days, and the in-between days. We can choose to be grateful for them all. You are passionate, peaceful, powerful, prosperous, and full of panache. Just like the lotus that would never bloom if it weren't for the mud it grows in, you are a beautiful flower who is meant to grow and bloom through it all.

Wishing you rainbows!

Acknowledgments

Each book I write is a dream come true, a wish fulfilled, a time capsule in which I lovingly tuck my intentions and insights inside of with the hope of inspiring, empowering, and transforming the reader. I am grateful to everyone who helped make this dream become a reality.

To my husband, Derek. You make me believe in magic. Thank you for stoking the initial spark of an idea I had for this book and for helping me manifest miracles daily. I'm in awe of the love we share and the life and business we're creating together.

To my mom, Judy. I am grateful for your early review of the manuscript, helpful feedback, and encouragement throughout the process of writing this book. Thank you for being a daily inspiration of a powerful, loving woman and the type of person I aspire to be.

To my sister, Julie. You are the sprinkles on the ice cream of my life. Thank you for your continual support for my crazy dreams and for always believing in me. You and Owen mean the world to me.

To my family. I appreciate your presence in my life and the experiences we've shared. I look forward to creating more magical, meaningful, and memorable adventures together in the future.

To my friend Ranj. I am grateful for your love, faith, friendship, and support. You continue to amaze me with all you create in your family, business, and community.

To my friend Shannon. Thank you for writing the foreword for my book and for being a beacon of light and love in the world.

To my editor, Lina. Thank you for helping to bring out the best in my writing and make this book everything I hoped it would be.

To you, my amazing Fans. I would like to express my love and gratitude for sharing this journey and spreading the love. Wishing you bliss!

About the Author

Sheri Fink is an inspirational speaker, #1 best-selling author, and president of Whimsical World, an innovative brand with a mission to inspire, delight, and educate children of all ages while planting seeds of self-esteem and high achievement. She is best known for her beloved "The Little Series" books, including *The Little Rose, The Little Unicorn,* and *The Little Dragon.*

An author of twelve best-selling books in multiple genres, Sheri travels the world inspiring audiences of all ages to believe in themselves, dream bigger dreams, and take action to live their best lives. Featuring her unique blend of empowerment and enthusiasm, she shares her inspirational journey along with strategies on overcoming adversity and how to live life with passion and aliveness. She has keynoted for some of the largest writers' conferences, women's organizations, and corporations in North America.

CBS Los Angeles selected Sheri as one of the top three authors in her local area, a distinction she shares with Dean Koontz. Her books have been honored with multiple awards, including three gold medals in the Readers' Favorite International Book Awards and four Gold Mom's Choice Awards, honoring the best in family-friendly entertainment.

She and her books have been featured in hundreds of articles, programs, websites, and shows, and her company was heralded as "An Empire to Inspire" by *Localista Magazine.* After being selected as a celebrity participant on Dancing with the South Bay Stars, she helped raise thousands of dollars for the South Bay Children's Health Center.

Sheri lives in Southern California where she makes dreams come true daily with her husband and their delightful dog, Zander. Discover more at SheriFink.com.

Recommended Resources

Podcasts
1. The Dave Ramsey Show – Practical financial advice for creating financial peace.
2. The Ranj Bawa Show – Insights about leadership, personal growth, and professional success.
3. The Clark Howard Show – Tips to strategically save and spend money on what matters.

Books

Passion
1. *The Passion Test: The Effortless Path to Discovering Your Life Purpose* by Janet Attwood and Chris Attwood
2. *The Five Love Languages* by Dr. Gary Chapman
3. *Untamed* by Glennon Doyle

Peace
1. *The Power of Now: A Guide to Spiritual Enlightenment* by Eckhart Tolle
2. *It's All Too Much: An Easy Plan for Living a Richer Life with Less Stuff* by Peter Walsh
3. *The Life-Changing Magic of Tidying Up: The Japanese Art of Decluttering and Organizing* by Marie Kondo

Power
1. *The Power of Focus* by Jack Canfield, Mark Victor Hansen, and Les Hewitt
2. *The Motivation Manifesto: 9 Declarations to Claim Your Personal Power* by Brendon Burchard
3. *How to Be a Bawse: A Guide to Conquering Life* by Lilly Singh

Prosperity
1. *The Total Money Makeover* by Dave Ramsey
2. *You Are a Badass at Making Money* by Jen Sincero

Panache
1. *Joy Seeker: Let Go of What's Holding You Back So You Can Live the Life You Were Made For* by Shannon Kaiser
2. *Simple Abundance: A Daybook of Comfort and Joy* by Sarah Ban Breathnach